Time Series Analysis and Adjustment

Time Series Analysis and Adjustment

Measuring, Modelling and Forecasting for Business and Economics

HAIM Y. BLEIKH
Taub Center for Social Policy Studies in Israel
and
WARREN L. YOUNG
Bar Ilan University, Israel

Routledge
Taylor & Francis Group
LONDON AND NEW YORK

First published 2014 by Gower Publishing

2 Park Square, Milton Park, Abingdon, Oxfordshire OX14 4RN
52 Vanderbilt Avenue, New York, NY 10017

Routledge is an imprint of the Taylor & Francis Group, an informa business

First issued in paperback 2020

Gower Applied Business Research
Our programme provides leaders, practitioners, scholars and researchers with thought provoking, cutting edge books that combine conceptual insights, interdisciplinary rigour and practical relevance in key areas of business and management.

British Library Cataloguing in Publication Data
A catalogue record for this book is available from the British Library.

ISBN 978-1-4094-4192-2 (hbk)
ISBN 978-0-367-66948-5 (pbk)

Library of Congress Cataloging-in-Publication Data
Bleikh, Haim Y.
Time series analysis and adjustment : measuring, modelling and forecasting for business and economics / by Haim Y. Bleikh and Warren L. Young.
pages cm
Includes bibliographical references and index.
ISBN 978-1-4094-4192-2 (hbk)
1. Economics--Mathematical models. 2. Time-series analysis. 3. Economic forecasting.
I. Young, Warren L., 1949- II. Title.
HB135.B565 2015
330.01'51955--dc23

2014005178

CONTENTS

LIST OF FIGURES

LIST OF TABLES

LIST OF ABBREVIATIONS

ACR	Autocorrelation
ACV	Autocovariance
ADF	Augmented Dickey Fuller
AIC	Akaike Information Criteria
AMB	ARIMA Model Based
AR	Autoregressive
ARI	Integrated Autoregressive
ARIMA	Autoregressive Integrated Moving Average
ARMA	Autoregressive Moving Average
BIC	Bayesian Information Criterion
BJ	Box and Jenkins
BK	Baxter and King
BN	Beveridge and Nelson
BO	Backshift Operator
CF	Christiano and Fitzgerald
CO	Cochrane-Orcutt
CPT	Cross Product Terms
DSP	Difference-Stationary Processes
DW	Durbin and Watson
ECM	Error Correction Model
HDE	Homogeneous Difference Equations
HP	Hodrick and Prescott
IMA	Integrated Moving Average
MA	Moving Average
MMSE	Minimum Mean Square Error
NP	Nelson and Plosser
OLS	Ordinary Lest-Squares
PACR	Partial Autocorrelation
PW	Prais-Winsten
PAT	Phase Average Trend
RegARIMA	Regression Models with ARIMA Errors
SAC	Sample Autocorrelation

SPAC	Sample Partial Autocorrelation
TSP	Trend-Stationary Processes
WN	White Noise
X-12	X-12-ARIMA
X-13-A-S	X-13-ARIMA Signal Extraction in Time Series
YW	Yule-Walker

INTRODUCTION

Time is a deceptive concept. Indeed, the study of time has interested mankind from the dawn of recorded history and probably before. Man has shown interest in both measuring the passage of time, and in understanding and explaining the occurrence of events at certain points in time. These events sometimes occurred repeatedly over time, or may have been distributed over time in a somewhat chaotic pattern. This led to the questions: *Why do these events have specific patterns of occurrence?* and *what can be learnt about future events, by observing their past?* Such questions arose in many disciplines, for instance, physics, meteorology, and even economics. Eventually, study of these phenomena, and the interest of people in understanding them, gave rise to a discipline known as *time series analysis*.

In this book, the prime concern is the analysis of *economic* time series and the application, and understanding, of related times series adjustment procedures. This is essential, and can be applied in different areas such as risk management, business cycle analysis, and forecasting etc. The study of economic time series, however, faces issues such as varying number of working and trading days in different months, movable national holidays etc. As a result, special attention must be given to such problems. However, the main problem in time series analysis is the problem of *randomness*. In real-life practice, data patterns are usually unclear, and we must not only attempt to uncover hidden patterns in the data, but also generate forecasts.

Much research has been conducted over the past decades to formalize, and model, different economic data and study contemporaneous relationship between variables. This field is known as *econometrics*. Concomitantly, a parallel stream of researchers from purely statistical and mathematical areas believed that economic theory is not strictly necessary for analysis of economic time series, and assumed that it would be better to allow the data to determine the model. These researchers became known as *time series analysts*. At first, there was little convergence between time series analysts and econometricians. However, since the 1970s this situation has greatly changed, and much convergence can be found between time series analysis and econometric approaches.

Unlike econometric methodology, research in time series analysis is concentrated on developing techniques for modeling time series and their components. In particular, time series analysts are concerned with the *decomposition* of a time series into a set of *unobserved components* and factors: *trend*, *cycle*, *seasonal* and *irregular*. Once the series is decomposed, analysis can be undertaken. Therefore, the choice and application of the *decomposition technique* has always been an important issue for most economic and financial institutions, and statistical bureaus.

The rapid rise of technology in different areas created the need for high speed computers, and along with this, a need for more sophisticated software and data analysis programs so as to enable the forecasting of time series. It must be emphasized, however, that a forecast made by a computer may not always be better than the prediction made by a person. Yet, no machine is able to change the human intuition, not to mention the accumulated professional experience by the person who analyzes the data. Nonetheless, as results can be obtained much faster by statistical software, it could, at first glance, be advantageous to sacrifice some accuracy if necessary. In addition, at least *statistically*, computer computations are usually more accurate than those made by humans.

The last four decades have brought dramatic changes in the way researchers analyze economic and financial data. The use of computers and computer software is *essential* for any modern quantitative analysis, and even more in time series analysis, where complex algorithms and extensive computations are often required. Indeed, the computation and understanding of the algorithms of modern time series programs can be a *difficult* or even an *impossible* task for the professional statistician, not to mention the statistically unsophisticated user. Nowadays, leading *time series programs* have *built-in automatic procedures* of *model selection*, *seasonal adjustment*, and time series *decomposition* into a set of *unobserved components*. Thus, users might have little, if any, influence at all, in the process of data *adjustment* for economic analysis. Automatic procedure is an important feature, from the point of view of many users of these programs. Nonetheless, understanding the programs' algorithm is an even more *crucial aspect*, especially when *different time series adjustment programs* are available, and each one may generate somewhat different results. This is the main reason why users of time series software *must* have a basic level of knowledge regarding *both theoretical* and *software* developments in this area.

This book examines the *history, evolution and recent developments in time series analysis and adjustment programs*. In particular, this work *combines* and surveys *both* elements – the *analytical* and the *programmatic*. It *also* provides information on the history of time series analysis, and on parallel developments related to *business cycles* analysis and *dynamic systems*. In addition, empirical analysis is conducted by means of the different time series analysis and adjustment methods that are discussed in the book.

There are two main reasons for an economist to study a time series: 1. *analysis*, i.e. ascertaining and summarizing the main properties of the time series; and 2. *modeling*, that is, in order to generate forecasts of the future values of the time series.

Over the last century, significant developments have taken place in the area of time series analysis and econometrics, respectively, albeit, separately. Only a few decades ago the *synthesis* between these approaches took place as a result of influential contributions made by Box and Jenkins, Granger and Newbold, and Beveridge and Nelson, among others. In addition, parallel developments in the area of time series *adjustment programs* have enabled the decomposition of time series into a set of *unobserved components* and factors: *trend*, *cycle*, *seasonal* and *irregular*. As a result, much knowledge and practical tools can be utilized by different specialists in different areas such as economics, physics, etc.

The aim of this book is to introduce the reader to both the history of time series analysis and to provide information for *practical* implementation of the leading procedures and methods for time series adjustment. The structure of the monograph is as follows. Chapters 1–4 provide the historical background to the development of time series analysis. In particular, it includes surveys of the influential approaches developed by Box and Jenkins, Granger and Newbold, Beveridge and Nelson, and Hodrick and Prescott, among others. Chapter 5 provides the background of developments in the area of time series adjustment programs, based on works of Shiskin, Dagum, Maravall and others. Chapter 6 provides an empirical analysis that includes a number of case studies. The aim of these case studies is to show that time series adjustment methods can be efficaciously applied and utilized, for both analysis and forecasting, albeit, they must be used in the context of reasoned statistical and economic judgment. There are also a number of methods whose mathematical developments are regarded as beyond the scope of this monograph, but computer programs are commonly available for their use.

The main conclusion of this book is that, while there is a diversification of modern methods of *time series analysis* and *adjustment* that can be utilized, *all must be utilized with judgment in practice, as different methods of analysis and adjustment may generate different statistical outcomes, especially in the short run.* The problem, however, is that such methods may require more than average time for research and analyses from different specialists. The main question which will be addressed in the future is: *if different organizations will go forward and utilize new methods or stay with old fashioned procedures?*

A list of relevant references is given in the end of this book, *and* in addition, mathematical and manipulative techniques are also discussed in detail in Appendices 1–3.

Finally, this book covers developments in time-series analysis and adjustment up to 2010. In such a dynamic field, things may change very rapidly. The reader is encouraged to check for the most recent developments in the field accordingly.

CHAPTER 1

LITERATURE SURVEY

The investigations of time series and seasonal adjustment methods have their origins in the nineteenth century. The idea that a time series is made up of both observed and unobserved components was known in scientific fields, such as astronomy and meteorology. In the middle of the nineteenth century, the Dutch meteorologist, Ballot, averaged temperature data for different periods of time (monthly, weekly etc.) in order to isolate individual periodic components that he assumed to be dependent upon astronomical factors, such as the moon's location (Grether and Nerlove, 1970).

At the beginning of the twentieth century, there was much research concerning seasonal adjustment. One of the most important works in the field was done by Persons in 1919 (Bell and Hillmer, 1984). He was probably among the first who came up with the idea of decomposition of time series into four components – *trend*, *cyclical*, *seasonal* and *irregular* components. Persons' method is known as the *link-relative method*, which isolated the components by utilizing de-trended and seasonally adjusted data to construct business indices. Despite the fact that Persons believed that seasonal variation is *not fixed* over time, in his methodological framework he utilized *fixed seasonal factors for adjustment of the data*. However, the use of *fixed* seasonal factors, as was suggested by Persons was argued by different researchers. It appears that the first researchers who introduced *varying seasonal factors* into seasonal adjustment procedure were Sydenstricker and Britten in 1922 (Fischer, 1995). However, it must be noted that the recognition of changing seasonality and its applications, had already been introduced in the nineteenth century by Gilbart in 1854, and at the beginning of the twentieth century, by Jevons in 1909 (see for example Grether and Nerlove, 1970; Bell and Hillmer, 1984). Persons' idea motivated others to continue research on the seasonal adjustment problem during the 1920s and in particular, these methods were proposed by other writers, such as Hall, Gressens, Clendenin, and Joy, and Thomas (Bell and Hillmer, 1984). In general, it was agreed that:

a) seasonality changes over time;
b) there is a need to account for trends and cycles when estimating the seasonal component;

c) trends and cycles cannot be described by mathematical formulae alone;
d) extreme observations had to be dealt with.

In 1931, Macauley suggested a procedure known as the *ratio to moving average method*, for seasonally adjusting data. This method was very important, since it became the basis for the Census Method 1 program, first introduced in 1954. Macauley's method was based on moving averages, rather than fitting explicit functions to the data, a technique that was borrowed from actuaries (see for example Shiskin et al., 1967, Hillmer et al., 1983).

On a parallel track, in the 1920s, the Russian mathematician and economist Slutzky, showed that utilizing a white noise sequence with a suitable weighting of random numbers, can create almost any pattern desired. There is, in fact, a theorem due to Slutzky (1937), which shows that, under certain conditions, repeated application of moving averages can eventually lead to a sequence that follows a sine wave. This is a highly important result, since it is well known that moving averages are applied in order to *smooth* the data, which indeed, can be said to be the exact opposite of Slutzky's results (Gilchrist, 1976). The models generated from this process are called *moving average models*, since they are created by *averaging white noise sequence*. At about the same time of Slutzky's work, Yule (1927) discovered the same fact, but by the reverse process. In particular, he showed that time series data could be described by a *linear aggregate of previous values of the process and a current error term*. These models are called *autoregressive models* (further discussion from the historical point of view of contributions of Slutzky and Yule can be found in Gottman, 1981).

During the 1950s and continuing over the next decades, in particular after the fundamental book of Burns and Mitchell (1946) at NBER, much attention had been addressed to analyzing business cycles and related macroeconomic factors. In their research, Burns and Mitchell concatenated a large number of *statistical indicators* of recessions and expansions into *one signal of turning points* in the US business cycle. However, their work led to methodological conflict, and in 1947 their work was highly criticized by Koopmans, a leading figure on the *Cowles Commission* and later Nobel Laureate. He wrote a review of Burns and Mitchell's book under the title *Measurement without Theory*. The review concentrated on the appropriate methodology for the analysis of business fluctuations. It opposed the NBER empirical approach, and refused to accept any theoretical basis for these statistical investigations (Malinvaud, 1983; Epstein, 1999). The stage was set, for the development of modern econometric analysis by distinguished researchers from *Cowles Commission*. This approach concentrated on the estimation of *simultaneous equations models*, *hypothesis testing* and *estimation by the maximum likelihood technique* etc. These results, for example, are collected in Hood and Koopmans (1953).

Since then, *different approaches* have been suggested to measure business cycles. In general, business cycles are fluctuations in output and employment about a *trend*. But, *what is a trend* and *how can we measure it?* These questions became important over time. A method which enjoyed great popularity among economists, assumed that a trend is a *deterministic function* of *time*. The cyclical component is simply the residual from a fitted trend line. The problem with this approach is "that the long-run evolution of the time series is deterministic and perfectly predictable" (Beveridge and Nelson, 1981: 152). Moreover, Zarnowitz and Ozyildirim (2002) asserted that too much of the overall variation is attributed to the business cycles. Thus, a linear trend does a poor job of distinguishing between good and bad economic periods over time. Another approach to measuring business cycles is known as *phase average trend* (PAT) method developed in NBER during the 1970s. This method is based on computing a centered 75 month moving average, which makes it necessary extrapolate backward/forward over first/last 37 months of the series covered. The use of moving average techniques in general generates an *end point* problem, but this is a common phenomenon with other methods as well (Zarnowitz and Ozyildirim, 2001).

Research on time series analysis was primarily concerned, on the other hand, with developing techniques for the decomposition of a time series into trend, cyclical seasonal and irregular components. Exponential smoothing proved through the years to be very useful in many analyses. These methods originated in the 1950s and 1960s with works of Holt (1957), Winters (1960) among other writers.

Until the late 1960s, there was *no synthesis* between econometric analysis and time series analysis, though famous works such as that of Cochrane-Orcutt (CO) (1949) and afterwards of Prais-Winsten (PW) (1954) had already been introduced in the econometric framework of time series regression. The works of CO and PW dealt with the *correction* of serial correlation in time series regression when there is non-zero autocorrelation between the successive errors.[1] On a parallel track, Durbin and Watson (DW) (1950, 1951), provided a test for *detecting* the existence of a first order serial correlation in the errors of the time series regression model. Later, Breusch (1978) and Godfrey (1978) developed a Lagrange Multiplier (LM) test that provided the econometricians with the ability to detect higher order autocorrelations.

However, this situation changed dramatically with publication of the volume by Box and Jenkins in 1970. The BJ approach is based on *autoregressive-integrated moving average* (ARIMA) processes. Their approach involves identifying an appropriate ARIMA process, fitting it to the data and finally using it for forecasting.

---

1 In such cases the OLS standard errors and test statistics are not valid. The main difference between CO and PW estimation depends on how the researcher deals with the first observation while treating the serial correlation problem.

One of the most important features of this approach is its ability to provide a model with an adequate description of the data.

Following the approach of Box and Jenkins, Beveridge and Nelson (1981) and Nelson and Plosser (1982) introduced new approaches related to the *definition of trend in analyzing business cycles.* The first approach defined trend as a *long-horizon forecast*, rather than one that is *fixed and pre-determined.* It implied that the trend *shifts* as new information (data) reveals more information about the future (Nelson, 2008). The second approach dealt with *trend-stationary* and *difference-stationary* processes which could be inferred from unit root analysis proposed by Dickey and Fuller (1979, 1981). In particular, it was argued by the writers that important economic aggregates have no tendency to return to a linear trend, suggesting that the trend is, rather stochastic.

As shown above, in the 1980s a sequence of influential papers dealt with measuring the macroeconomic variables in the context of business cycles. Another popular approach to the measurement of business cycles is the Hodrick and Prescott (HP) filter (1980, 1997). Indeed, Prescott wrote:

> Our trend is just a well-defined statistic, where a statistic is a real valued function. Hodrick and Prescott's trend statistic mimics well the smooth curve that economists fit through the data ... A desirable feature of this definition is that with the selection of smoothing parameters for quarterly time series, there are no degrees of freedom and the business cycle statistics are not a matter of judgment (2004: 377).

As it is well known, *seasonally adjusted data* provides more interpretable measures of changes occurring in a given period, and reflects real economic movements without problematic seasonal changes. The *choice* of method for seasonal adjustment is crucial for the removal of *all* seasonal effects in the data. Thus, in 1954 the US Census Bureau released its first computer program for seasonal adjustment – Census Method 1. Over the years this program underwent different modifications. The last version of this program was called X-11 (Shiskin et al., 1967). In the mid-1970s Statistics Canada developed the X-11-ARIMA program, which was based on X-11 and the approach of Box and Jenkins (Dagum, 1978). The latter program, also underwent modifications, leading to the version known as X-11-ARIMA/88. During the 1990s US Census Bureau developed a new seasonal adjustment program, X-12-ARIMA, while another program in common use is the TRAMO/SEATS package, developed by the Bank of Spain (further discussion about the evolution of program methods will be discussed in Chapter 5).

The counter-argument to the utilization of seasonally adjusted data in macro-economic analysis, is derived from the fact that seasonally adjusted data do not provide consistently improved predictions, and in many cases forecasts based upon them are even less accurate than those derived from non-seasonally adjusted data. Comparative analyses related to this issue is well established in the literature and can be found, for example, in Makridakis and Hibon (1979), Plosser (1979), and Moosa and Ripple (2000). Yet, no clear cut answer is provided, as it is argued for example, by Bell and Hillmer (1984).

Throughout the years different studies dealt with the fundamental question: does it make sense to utilize filtered data? For example, Lee and Siklos (1993) tested the permanent income hypothesis (PIH) using Canadian data. Their results supported the PIH for filtered data, but not in the case where the data was not filtered. In the study conducted by Meyer and Winker (2005), a Monte Carlo simulation was performed in order to examine the performance of the *HP filtered* and *non-filtered* data in a regression framework. Their results suggested that estimates of an econometric model may be distorted by utilization of filtered data. As Nelson and Kang (1981: 742) pointed out in their paper that discussed the influence of the detrended data utilized for econometric analysis: "… the dynamics of econometric models estimated from such data may well be wholly or in part an artifact of the trend removal procedure".

Looking back at literature, seasonal adjustment procedures were discussed in different papers. For example, Rosenblatt (1968) and Grether and Nerlove (1970) discussed the utilization of the spectral analysis when dealing with seasonally adjusting data. On the other hand, seasonal adjustment by regression analysis was discussed in Lovell (1963), Thomas and Wallis (1971) and Sims (1974).

It must be emphasized that the statistical method of time series analysis deals with univariate processes, as it is discussed in Box and Jenkins (1970). However, a substantial part of macroeconomic analysis deals with multivariate relationships. The cooptation of this statistical method into dynamic macroeconomic systems was implemented in the contributions of Granger (1969), Granger and Weiss (1983) and Engle and Granger (1987) (further discussion is given in Chapter 4).

During the 1990s, a number of important developments occurred in the area of filtering, followed the work of Hodrick and Prescott. New filters were created by Baxter and King (BK) (1995) and Christiano and Fitzgerald (CF) (1999). These filters formulate the de-trending and smoothing problem in the *frequency domain*. A number of empirical studies used different filters, and compared the results obtained. For example, Demertzis and Hallet (2003) and Montoya and de Haan (2007) compared CF with HP, while Guay and St-Amant (1997, 2005) provided analysis of BK and HP.

Recent developments in time series analysis and seasonal adjustment procedures are concentrated in the combination of X-12-ARIMA and SEATS. In 2006, the US Census Bureau with the support of Bank of Spain released a new program which is called X-13-ARIMA-SEATS. This program offers the user the seasonal adjustment of *both methods,* with improved diagnostics for the model-based seasonal adjustments (Monsell, 2006; Findley, 2005; Monsell, Aston and Koopman, 2003).

CHAPTER 2

FORECASTING

2.1 FORECASTING: IMPORTANCE AND LIMITATIONS

The choice and application of the proper forecast technique has always been an important issue for most economic and financial institutions, and statistical bureaus. At the micro-level of the firm, an entire financial operation may rely on the accuracy of the forecasts since such information will likely be used to make interrelated decisions in areas of budgeting, purchasing, marketing and advertising, capital financing, personnel management, etc. Moreover, at the macro-level of the economy as a whole, forecast accuracy can also be crucial. For example, at the firm level, a significant over-sales forecast error may cause the firm to be burdened with excess inventory carrying costs. On the other hand, an under-sales forecast can create a loss of sales revenue. During periods when demand is fairly stable, or is unchanging or growing, or on the other hand, declining at a known constant rate, making an accurate forecast is less difficult. If, on the other hand, during its history, the firm has experienced an up-and-down sales pattern, then the forecasting task can be rather complicated. At the macroeconomic level, a shortfall in tax revenue, despite a forecast to the contrary, can lead to a budget deficit, and the consequences that follow from it.

Many everyday decisions, both professional and personal are made intuitively. This often happens when a short term response is under consideration and no time and/or resources are available for a sophisticated analysis of the data. Moreover, the decision maker may believe that his intuition, in particular, is more trustworthy than any mathematical forecasting model. The most important characteristic of this kind of intuitive model is that it is not reproducible. We can, however, understand how the intuitive decision-making process works, by interviewing the forecaster and by examining previous forecasts. In this case, it seems that we are dealing with a kind of a "black box".

As was previously mentioned, time and resources are crucial for decision making.[1]

1 The selection of the model that the organization might utilize involves trade-offs between time, costs, and desired forecast accuracy. The construction of a structural model can

Ideally, organizations which can afford to do so, will usually assign crucial forecast responsibilities to those departments and/or individuals that are best qualified and have the necessary resources at hand to make such forecast estimations under complicated demand patterns. Clearly, a firm with a large ongoing operation and a technical staff composed of statisticians, management scientists, computer analysts, etc., is in a much better position to select and make proper use of sophisticated forecasting techniques than a company with more limited resources.

Consider the case when the resources are available. In that case, the organization might choose to employ some mathematical and statistical models to implement the forecasting process. One such method is to build a structural model that consists of casual relationships that represent the organization's environment. In other words, it is necessary to decide on the factors that coexist in the system, where they are represented as a set of functions. Once the set of functions are mathematically defined, and parameter inference is dealt with, the model can be estimated. Certainly, no data can fit all kinds of equations. Therefore, it is acceptable to add to the model a random variable with a mean of zero, namely "unobserved disturbances". This random variable is important since it allows the model to absorb inevitable deviations. Such structural models are referred to "econometric models", and the estimation of the parameters is a problem in the application of the theory of econometrics.

The information provided by the forecasting process can be utilized in many ways. An important concern in forecasting is the problem of evaluating the nature of the forecast error, by using the appropriate statistical tests. For example, in the single-equation regression model, ordinary lest-squares (OLS) estimation yields the best forecast among all linear unbiased estimators having minimum mean-square error (Maddala, 2001). With respect to the error, it is important to mention its sources. The error associated with a forecasting procedure can result from a combination of a number of factors. First, the random nature of the future values of independent variables guarantees that forecasts will deviate from true values, even if the model is specified correctly, and its parameter values are known. Second, realized values of future disturbances will not necessary equal zero. Third, the forecast error might be affected by the "sampling error" present in estimates of the parameters.[2] Fourth,

require large expenditures of time and money. The gains from this effort may include a better understanding of the relationships and structure involved as well as the ability to make a better forecast. However, in some cases, these gains may be so small as to be outweighed by the heavy costs involved. Because a structural model demands a good deal of knowledge about the process being studied, the construction of such models may be extremely complicated.

2 Sampling errors arise from estimating a population characteristic by looking at only one portion of the population rather than the entire population. It refers to the difference between the estimate derived from a sample survey and the "true" value that would result if a census

the question that concerns us dealing with exogenous variables remains open.[3] Yet, many other important determinants will remain unknown until future periods. Finally, errors may be introduced because the model specification may not be an accurate representation of the "true" model.

2.2 FORECASTING MODELS: A BRIEF REVIEW

In physical processes, for example, when tracking missiles, the proper model that represents reality is obvious. However, this may not be the case when dealing with economic forecasting. There are too many complicated factors, with complex interactions, to allow derivation of an equation that describes the process underlying the observed data. In these cases, we should choose a descriptive model that approximates local sections of the observed time series well enough to get a useful forecast. In this chapter we will present several models used for forecasting. We first turn to mathematically-based *curve-fitting forecasting models*, and then to *structural* and *probability models.*

Curve-fitting Models

Constant mean models In this case the underlying process does not change over time. This process can be modeled as follows: $y_t = x_t + \varepsilon_t$ where ε_t is a *white noise* (WN), with a zero mean and constant variance. The values of time series appear to be random samples that have been independently derived from some distribution, with a mean and variance that does not change over time. In this case, the future observation will be derived from the same distribution, and the forecast to use for this process will be the sample mean, i.e. the forecast equation will be: $\hat{y}_t = \bar{x}$.

Linear time-trend models In this case the model is $y_t = a + bt + \varepsilon_t$, i.e. a model with an upward or downward trend, where ε_t is WN. Again, we can never know the true value of a and b, thus are required to estimate them. Hence, the estimated equation will be: $\hat{y}_t = \hat{a} + \hat{b}t$.

Polynomial models In such cases a quadratic representation is used such as: $y_t = a + bt + ct^2 + \varepsilon_t$, i.e. polynomial of second degree.[4] If the coefficient c>0, then the trend is shifting from downward to upward. When c<0, the trend is shifting from an upward to downward direction.

---

of the whole population were taken under the same conditions. There are no sampling errors in a census because the calculations are based on the entire population.

3 The statistical or econometric concept emphasizes non correlation between the exogenous variable and other independent variables included in the model.

4 In general, the highest exponent in the model determines the degree of the polynomial.

Exponential models An exponential function describes a process where the rate of growth is proportional to the state of growth. The change in value from one observation can be expressed as a constant percentage of the current value. These models are used, for example, in many areas from population to finance. Such a process can be formulated as follows: $y_t = ae^{kt}$.

Cyclical-periodic (trigonometric-fitted) models Generally speaking a function is said to be periodic if for $p > 0$, $f(x) = f(x + p)$, i.e. these functions repeat over and over, or cycle on a specified period. In such cases, it is appropriate to describe the data in terms of sines and cosines. Let us consider an example. The height of a tide may be observed once an hour. Starting at high tide, the heights decrease for six hours and then start to rise again. Twelve hours later, the heights will start to go through the same sequence again. This is a process with a period of twelve hours, which can be described as follows: $y_t = a\cos(2\pi t / 12)$, where t is measured in hours, starting at high tide and y_t is the departure from average level.

Structural Models

Regression models These statistical models describe the variation in one or more dependent variable(s) when one or more other variable(s) vary. Inference based on such models is known as regression analysis. Generally such a process is described by:

$$y(x) = \sum_{i=1}^{n} a_i f_i(x_i)$$

where the functions $f_i(x_i)$ can be any arbitrary function.[5]

Despite the wide use of such models, we must emphasize two points when using regression models. The first point concerns the validity of the model. The first step in regression analysis is estimating the functional relationship between the dependent variable and the independent variable or variables, given that there is no multicollinearity.[6] After the step of estimating the parameters we reach the forecasting stage. If the forecast is done within the range of values of the variables used to construct the model, this is known as *in period forecasting*.[7] Forecasting outside the range of the data used to construct the model is known as *outside period forecasting*. The second point relates to the interpretation of conclusions

---

5 For example, $y(x) = a_1 x_1^2 + a_2 e^{x_2}$, where $f_1(x_1) = x_1^2$ and $f_2(x_2) = e^{x_2}$.

6 Multicollinearity refers to a situation in which two or more independent (explanatory) variables in a multiple regression model are highly correlated.

7 Determination of values that lie between the known values is known as interpolation. The simplest case is the linear interpolation where the missing point is a linear combination of the given data points. On the other hand, the prediction of values beyond the given range of data is known as extrapolation. The methods of extrapolation are similar to those of interpolation.

drawn from a regression model and its forecasts. It is sometimes tempting to interpret a relationship in a regression model as if changing the independent variable(s) is the reason for change in the dependent variable, i.e., that change in the independent variables causes a change in the dependent variable. But a regression model does not say anything about causation. It simply states that if the value of the independent variable(s) changes, the value of the dependent variable also changes. There can be a number of reasons for an observed relationship. One possibility is that changes in the independent variable do cause changes in the dependent variable. But who can guarantee that the opposite is not the case, that is, changes in the dependent variable are the reason for changes in the independent variable(s). Furthermore, changes in a third variable could be a good explanation for changes in both the dependent and the independent variable(s). Finally, there is also a possibility that the observed relationship is a coincidence, that is, if it is simply due to random variation.

To conclude, the motivation behind trying to specify the most accurate descriptive economic model arises from the desire to produce accurate forecasts. Unfortunately, the accuracy of an economic forecast is not easy to judge. There are simply too many dimensions of detail and interest. Concomitantly, self-judgment of the economist is an integral part of the forecasting process. As Hymans wrote:

> Econometric forecasting is the joint product of the econometric model and the economist who uses it. Studies have shown that forecasts that combine the model and the forecaster's judgment are generally more accurate than "purely objective" forecasts that are produced with the econometric model alone.[8]

Advanced technology has made forecasting models more precise than ever before. And, while not a perfect system, econometric forecasting models provide important information for the consumer, business, and government alike.

Probability Models

A probability model is a mathematical representation of a random phenomenon. It is defined by its sample space, events within the sample space, and probabilities associated with each event.

Usually, when thinking about forecasting we tend to focus on time series models. In some situations, the pattern of the process over the time period is more relevant. However, there are situations where the shape of the probability distribution, from which the observations are taken, is of more concern than the shift in the outcome

8 *Forecasting and Econometric Models*, 1st edition, by Saul H. Hymans. See http://www.econlib.org/

itself.[9] Let us consider such an example. A businessman must arrive on time for a crucial meeting at his office at 9.00 a.m., and being late, is unthinkable. He knows that the bus leaves the station, at exactly 8.15 a.m., and he also knows, according to its schedule, it arrives at 8:55 a.m. It also takes him about two minutes to cross the street, and finally enter his office. His alternative is taking a taxi. However, from his daily experience, there are sometimes deviations from the scheduled arrival time of the bus, that is, the man has "built up" some sort of estimate of this probability distribution. Indeed, the average forecast in this case, is that this man should arrive on time. But will this forecast be good enough for him, to make the right decision? We shall leave this question open.

An important aspect which has to be emphasized when dealing with probability distribution is the fact that it changes slowly with time. On the other hand, in our example, it is enough to add another traffic light and we might have a different shape of the distribution.

We conclude by emphasizing an important implication of a probability forecast, that is using probability methods have no such clear sense of "right" and "wrong". Thus, the fact that on any given forecast day, two forecasters arrive at different subjective probabilities from the same data, does not mean that one is right and the other wrong. It simply means that one is more certain of the event than the other. Therefore, a statement such as "the probability of a power outage is between 0.3 and 0.4" is more natural and realistic than their exact counterpart such as "the probability of a power outage is 0.3541".

---

9 The concept of probability occupies an important place in the decision-making process in different fields such as business, government, social sciences, or just in one's own everyday personal life. In a very few decision-making situations we deal with perfect information, i.e., all the needed facts are available. Most decisions are made in the face of uncertainty. Probability enters into the process by playing the role of a substitute for certainty – a substitute for complete knowledge.

CHAPTER 3

UNIVARIATE TIME SERIES ANALYSIS

3.1 ARIMA MODEL BUILDING – THE BOX-JENKINS (BJ) APPROACH

Modeling and forecasting procedures involve knowledge about the mathematical model of a process. However, in practice, data patterns are unclear, individual observations involve considerable error, and we need to uncover not only hidden patterns in the data, but also, to generate forecasts. The *ARIMA methodology* developed by Box and Jenkins (1970) allows us to do just that, that is, we can explain the behavior of the time series by, a *combination of past movements* in the series itself, and a *white noise sequence* (Young, 1977). The BJ approach attained popularity in many areas, and research practice confirmed its power and flexibility. In particular, one of the attractive features of the BJ approach is a very rich class of possible models, and it is usually possible to find one that can provide an adequate description of the time series process. Nonetheless, the high flexibility of the BJ approach requires a great deal of experience on the part of researchers, since it is a complex technique.

In this chapter, we briefly review the main steps in the BJ approach. We first introduce the approach in the context of *non-seasonal time series*. Afterwards, the discussion will include *seasonal time series.* A detailed discussion of the BJ approach, and in particular, examples of well-recognized time series processes, and their related features, are given in Appendices 1–3. Discussion can be also found in volumes such as, those of Box and Jenkins (1970), Nelson (1973), Nazem (1988) among other texts.

3.2 GENERAL NON-SEASONAL BJ MODEL

The first step in BJ approach is to determine if the time series is stationary. BJ recommend differencing *non-stationary* series one or more times to achieve stationarity. More specifically: (1) $w_t = (1-B)^d y_t$, where y_t – the original time series; $B^j y_t = y_{t-j}$; d – stands for the degree of differencing the time series. Thus, the following ARMA process can be given by (2) $a_p(B)w_t = b_q(B)\varepsilon_t$, where:

$a_p(B) = (1 - a_1 B - \ldots - a_p B^p)$, p – is the degree of the autoregressive (AR) process;

$b_q(B) = (1 - b_1 B - \ldots - b_q B^q)$, q – is the degree of the moving average (MA) process;

ε_t is WN.

The combination of (1) and (2) gives us the general BJ model for *non-seasonal* time series: (3) $(1 - a_1 B - \ldots - a_p B^p)(1 - B)^d y_t = \delta + (1 - b_1 B - \ldots - b_q B^q)\varepsilon_t$ or in short $a_p(B)(1 - B)^d y_t = \delta + b_q(B)\varepsilon_t$, δ – is the long run mean of the time series. As is well known, the latter equation is referred to an ARIMA process of order (p,d,q). The *stationarity* and *invertibility* conditions are satisfied if the *roots* of: $(1 - a_1 B - \ldots - a_p B^p) = 0$ and $(1 - b_1 B - \ldots - b_q B^q) = 0$ *lie outside the unit circle.* Practically speaking, the latter condition is related to the values of the model parameters, $a's$ and $b's$, that is, we require that $|a_i| < 1$ for $i = 1, 2 \ldots p$ and $|b_j| < 1$ for $j = 1, 2 \ldots q$.

There are four primary stages in building and assessing BJ time series model.

1. Identification.
2. Estimation.
3. Diagnostics.
4. Forecasting.

Stage 1 – Model Identification: Correlogram and Partial Correlogram

Since the class of ARIMA models is a rich one, the answer to the question which *p, d* and *q* parameters should be chosen, can be rather a complicated one. To answer this question, BJ suggested an examination of the *autocorrelation* and partial *correlation functions* as an identification procedure. Practically, we do not know the real autocorrelation and partial correlation functions. Therefore, we must estimate them on the basis of the data. Thus, the *sample autocorrelation* (SAC) and *sample partial autocorrelation* (SPAC) functions are expressed as follows:

$$\text{SAC} - \hat{\rho}_k = \frac{\sum_{t=k+1}^{n} (y_t - \bar{y})(y_{t-k} - \bar{y})}{\sum_{t=1}^{n} (y_t - \bar{y})^2}, \; k = 1,2\ldots$$

SPAC of order k between y_t and y_{t-k} is given by a_{kk}, and derived from the next equation: $\hat{\rho}_j = \hat{a}_{k1}\hat{\rho}_{j-1} + \hat{a}_{k2}\hat{\rho}_{j-2} + \ldots + \hat{a}_{kk}\hat{\rho}_{j-k}$ where k is the order of the AR process. In general, a_{kk}, can be obtained from the *Yule-Walker* (YW) equations as it is discussed in Appendix 3. The results of both SAC and SPAC should be examined from the graphical representation, i.e., from examining the correlogram and partial correlogram. For example, different results are given next:

- AR(1): SAC – exponential decay; SPAC – spike at lag 1, no correlation for other lags.
- AR(2): SAC – a sine-wave shape pattern or a set of exponential decays; SPAC – spikes at lags 1 and 2, no correlation for other lags.
- MA(1): SAC – spike at lag 1, no correlation for other lags; SPAC – damps out exponentially.
- MA(2): SAC – spikes at lags 1 and 2, no correlation for other lags; SPAC – a sine-wave shape pattern or a set of exponential decays.
- ARMA(1,1): SAC – exponential decay starting at lag 1; SPAC – exponential decay starting at lag 1.

Stage 2 – Estimation

For pure AR models, there exist simple estimation techniques, since there are linear relationships between the autocorrelations and the AR parameters. In general for the AR(p) model $y_t = a_1 y_{t-1} + a_2 y_{t-2} + \ldots. + \varepsilon_t$ we obtain a *system of YW equations*, if we (a) multiply both sides of the equation by y_{t-k} $(k = 1, 2 \ldots p)$; (b) take expectations. The k'th equation in the system of the YW equations is given next:

$$\rho_k - a_1\rho_{k-1} + a_2\rho_{k-2} + \ldots a_p\rho_{k-p}$$

Again, we do not know the real parameters of the model and the system of YW equations. Therefore, we use the estimates that are given next:

$$\hat{\rho}_k = \hat{a}_1\hat{\rho}_{k-1} + \hat{a}_2\hat{\rho}_{k-2} + \ldots + \hat{a}_p\hat{\rho}_{k-p}$$

For the MA models, estimation is rather different, and considerably more complicated. Nonetheless, the existence of the invertibility condition, *which inverts the MA process into an infinite AR process*, allows us to solve this problem.

To conclude, the estimating procedure of the parameters for the BJ models is a quite complicated non-linear estimation problem. For this reason, the parameter estimation should be left to high quality software programs. Fortunately, many commercial statistical software programs now fit BJ models. The main approaches to fitting BJ models are *non-linear least squares* and *maximum likelihood estimation.*

Stage 3 – Diagnostics

Once the model parameters are estimated, the standard errors and confidence intervals are derived. Thus, the significance of the parameters can be examined accordingly. However, it is highly recommended to estimate a more general model, that is, to add more parameters to the model and check its significance. BJ called that procedure *over-fitting*.

The most commonly used method is examining the behavior of the *residuals* of the *fitted model*. In particular, we have to check the correlogram of these residuals and see if they correspond to a WN sequence. Box and Pierce (1970) suggested a *portmanteau* statistics that is computed as the weighted sum of squares of a sequence of *residual autocorrelations*, as follows:

$$Q = T\sum_{k=1}^{m} r_k^2(\hat{\varepsilon})$$

where m is usually at least 20. The model is said to be inadequate if the Q statistic exceeds the tabulated value distributed as χ^2 with $(m-p-q)$degrees of freedom. However, questions have been raised with respect to the Q statistic as proposed by Box and Pierce. Davies, Triggs and Newbold (1977) argued that even for quite large samples, the true significant levels for the Q statistic could be much smaller than was initially proposed. In other words, very often a number of models satisfy the diagnostic test, despite the fact that not *all* of these models are necessarily appropriate for the sample data. As a result, Ljung and Box (1978) suggested a new statistic which is given by:

$$Q^* = T(T+2)\sum_{k=1}^{m} \frac{r_k^2(\hat{\varepsilon})}{T-k}$$

which is nowadays one of the main tests in the computer programs. Nazem (1988) analyzed 84 time series and the result indicated that the existence of different adequate models for a time series can be quite a common phenomenon. This result is very important from a practitioner's point of view. *It suggests that the use of diagnostic Q^* statistic performs well, but it should be used with caution.*

Stage 4 – Forecasting

We know that the general ARIMA process can be given by:

$$(1) \quad a_p(B)\nabla^d y_t = \delta + b_q(B)\varepsilon_t$$

Since $a_p(B)\nabla^d = c(B) = 1 - c_1B - c_2B^2 \ldots - c_{p+d}B^{p+d}$, we then obtain:

$$(2) \quad y_t = \delta + c_1 y_{t-1} + c_2 y_{t-2} + \ldots + c_{p+d} y_{t-p-d} \ldots + \varepsilon_t - b_1 \varepsilon_{t-1} - b_2 \varepsilon_{t-2} - \ldots b_q \varepsilon_{t-q}$$

Following (2), we have (3) $y_{t+1} = \delta + c_1 y_t + \ldots c_{p+d} y_{t-p-d+1} + \varepsilon_{t+1} - b_1 \varepsilon_t - \ldots b_q \varepsilon_{t-q+1}$ (shifted forward one period). The forecast of y_{t+1} is defined as a linear combination of the past and present values of $y's$, which can be regarded as conditional expectation of y_{t+1}, given y_t, y_{t-1}..., or in short $E(y_{t+1}|\Omega_t) = \hat{y}_t(1)$. Thus, a *one-step ahead forecast*, is given by:

$$(4) \quad \hat{y}_t(1) = \delta + c_1 y_t + \ldots c_{p+d} y_{t-p-d+1} - b_1 \varepsilon_t - \ldots b_q \varepsilon_{t-q+1}$$

Indeed (3) and (4) look similar, except for ε_{t+1}, the disturbance. In particular, from (4), we have $E(\varepsilon_{t+1}|\Omega_t) = 0$, while, the rest of the variables from period t and *prior* to it, are already realized. This implies that $y_t - \hat{y}_{t-1}(1) = \varepsilon_t$ or, more generally, $y_{t-i} - \hat{y}_{t-i-1}(1) = \varepsilon_{t-i}$ for $i = 0, 1, 2\ldots$. In addition, $\hat{y}_t(1)$ can be shown to be the *minimum mean square error* (MMSE) forecast of y_{t+1}, made at time t.

Following the mechanism of *one-step ahead forecasting*, the *multi-step ahead forecast* is given as follows:

$$(5) \quad E(y_{t+k}|\Omega_t) = \hat{y}_t(k) = \delta + c_1 E(y_{t+k-1}|\Omega_t) + \ldots c_{p+d} E(y_{t-p-d+k}|\Omega_t) - b_1 \varepsilon_t - \ldots b_q \varepsilon_{t-q+k}$$

It appears that the forecast can be computed using the recursive method as follows:

$$\hat{y}_t(1) = \delta + c_1 y_t + \ldots c_{p+d} y_{t-p-d+1} - b_1 \varepsilon_t - \ldots b_q \varepsilon_{t-q+1}$$

$$\hat{y}_t(2) = \delta + c_1 E(y_{t+1}|\Omega_t) + c_2 y_{t+2} \ldots c_{p+d} y_{t-p-d+2} - b_1 \varepsilon_t - \ldots b_q \varepsilon_{t-q+2}$$

$$\vdots$$

where the replacement of the values should be subject to the conditions:

$$E(y_{t+k}|\Omega_t) = \begin{Bmatrix} y_{t+k}, & k \le 0 \\ \hat{y}_t(k), & k > 0 \end{Bmatrix} \quad \text{and} \quad E(\varepsilon_{t+k}|\Omega_t) = \begin{Bmatrix} \varepsilon_{t+k}, & k \le 0 \\ 0, & k > 0 \end{Bmatrix}$$

For further discussion, see Box and Jenkins (1970), Nelson (1973), Mills (1990) among other text books. Examples of BJ forecasting are given in Chapter 6.

3.3 EXTENSIONS OF THE BJ APPROACH

Originally, Box and Jenkins proposed that their method could be extended to encompass bivariate analysis by using a "transfer function-noise model" approach. In this case, we suppose that the variable Y_t is dependent on X_t, so that $Y_t = \alpha + \beta X_t + u_t$, where u_t is the error term. We obtain the estimates $\hat{u}_t$ and $r_K(\hat{u}_t)$ for $k = 1, 2 \ldots$

under the condition that $u_t = 1/(1-\varphi B)a_t$, where a_t is white noise. We then suppose that $\hat{u}_t$ and u_t have approximately the same auto-correlation structure, so that we obtain, by substitution:

$$Y_t = \alpha + bX_t + (1/1-\varphi B)\, a_t$$

which, after transformation, yields:

$$Y_t = \varphi Y_{t-1} + \alpha(1-\varphi B) + \beta(X_t - \varphi X_{t-1}) + a_t$$

The approach can be extended, therefore, to multivariate analysis, but the estimation of parameters would, in this case, prove difficult. Box and Jenkins outlined a detailed strategy for building bivariate transfer function type models, while work done by Granger and Newbold extended the BJ approach to the multivariate case (Box and Cox, 1964; Box and Jenkins, 1968; Granger and Newbold, 1976).

The BJ approach was also used to deal with the effects of "interventions" on a response variable given a dependent noise structure. In this regard, Box and Tiao (1975) utilized such an approach – which they called "intervention analysis" – in an attempt to answer questions of the type: "given a known intervention, is there evidence that change in the series of the kind expected actually occurred, and, if so, what can be said of the nature and magnitude of the change?"

Glass (1972, 1975), who introduced the term "intervention", applied, along with others, the BJ approach in order to analyze structural changes and non-stationarity in time series. These researchers found that the BJ framework was quite applicable to these types of problems. This resulted from the fact that procedures such as the "t test" for estimating mean changes due to an intervention were not applicable to time series, since these were often serially correlated, and exhibited non-stationarity, in addition to occasionally reflecting seasonality. As such, parametric or non-parametric tests which depended on normality, constant variance, and independence of the observations, were of no use in this case, while those relying on the independence or symmetry of distribution where neither available nor random in nature. Box and Tiao concluded, therefore, the models based on ARIMA methodology which they proposed to use in intervention analysis could readily be extended to represent many situations of potential interest (1975: 70–72).

3.4 SEASONAL TIME SERIES AND BJ ANALYSIS

Most forecasting activity in economics and business is based on quarterly, monthly and even weekly estimates of future movements. "Seasonality means a tendency to repeat a pattern of behavior over a seasonal period, generally one year" (Nelson,

1973: 168). It is well known, that many reported time series are *seasonally adjusted*. In general, seasonal adjustment refers to a *smoothing procedure*, that is, it involves the process of *estimating* and *removing* the seasonal effects from a time series. Further discussion on seasonal adjustment techniques and programs will be presented below.

In general, there are two kinds of *seasonal effects* in time series data. The first is known as the *deterministic seasonal effect*. It appears at regular intervals of time with some precisely measurable force. Such force can either increase or decrease over the years, but the changes possess a regular pattern that can be determined from historical data. The second seasonal effect is known as the *probabilistic* one. It does not possess any definite pattern, but nonetheless, occurs at regular intervals or seasonally (Nazem, 1988). Thus, the main interest of economists is to find a solution that incorporates these seasonal phenomena, so that future seasonal effects could be reflected in the forecasting procedure.

3.5 BJ SEASONAL MODELS

In general, seasonality can be observed from a time series plot and observing the correlogram of the initial time series. In particular, the SAC usually produces a very distinct pattern that repeats every k lags. The elimination of seasonal component is achieved through differencing the data with the appropriate *span of seasonality*. For instance, if the time series, y_t, is quarterly, then a new series can be defined as follows: $z_t = y_{t+4} - y_t$ for $t = 1, 2, ...T-4$. In the compact general form, it can be represented as $z_t = (1 - B^s)y_t = \nabla_s^D y_t$ where s is the span of seasonality, which equals 4 or 12 for quarterly and monthly data, respectively.[1]

The BJ approach to seasonal time series involves almost the same procedures as required in non-seasonal time series. The main difference lies in the span of seasonality, namely seasonal differencing. Thus, for example, *stochastic seasonal* models could be expressed by pure AR and pure MA models as follows:

(a) *Pure* seasonal *AR*: $y_t = a_s y_{t-s} + ... + a_{Ps} y_{t-Ps} + \varepsilon_t$, and if $A_j = a_{js}$ then we obtain: $y_t = A_1 y_{t-s} + ... + A_P y_{t-Ps} + \varepsilon_t$, or in the compact version we can rewrite it as $\varepsilon_t = A_P(B^s)y_t$ where $A_P(B^s) = 1 - A_1 B^s - ... - A_P B^{Ps}$.

(b) *Pure* seasonal *MA*: $y_t = c_s \varepsilon_{t-s} + ... + c_{Qs} y_{t-Qs} + \varepsilon_t$, and if $C_j = c_{js}$ then we obtain: $y_t = C_1 \varepsilon_{t-s} + ... + C_Q \varepsilon_{t-Qs} + \varepsilon_t$, or in the compact version we can rewrite it as $y_t = C_Q(B^s)\varepsilon_t$, where $C_Q(B^s) = 1 - C_1 B^s - ... - C_Q B^{Qs}$.

1 Note that ∇^d refers to non-seasonal differencing whereas ∇_s^D indicates seasonal differencing.

3.6 GENERAL MULTIPLICATIVE MODEL: AN EXAMPLE

If we look at the data shown in the *table of retail* sales below, we might find a seasonal pattern for a particular quarter.[2] For example, Q4 is related to previous observation of Q4's in different years. Hence BJ suggested a model which can link the observations of each quarter as follows:

(1) $A_P(B^s)\nabla_s^D y_t = C_Q(B^s)v_t$, where y_t is the t'th observation in Q4; $A_P(B^s)$ and $C_Q(B^s)$ are polynomials of degree P and Q which satisfy the stationarity and invertibility conditions, respectively. Now, suppose that the same formulation holds for every quarter. This implies that errors from a fixed quarter in different years are uncorrelated. However, the errors corresponding to the adjacent observations in the same year need not in general be uncorrelated, for example, retails sales in 1958 Q4 will also be related to the values from 1958 Q3, 1958 Q2 and so on. Therefore, the errors which are given by $v_t, v_{t-1}...$ *may be autocorrelated.* Thus, these autocorrelations may be expressed by a non-seasonal ARIMA (p,d,q) model:

(2) $a(B)\nabla^d v_t = b(B)\varepsilon_t$, where ε_t is WN process, $a(B)$ and $b(B)$ are polynomials of degrees p and q respectively, satisfying the stationarity and invertibility conditions. As a result, if we combine (1) and (2), we obtain a general *multiplicative seasonal model*:

(3) $a_p(B)A_P(B^s)\nabla^d\nabla_s^D y_t = b_q(B)C_Q(B^s)\varepsilon_t$, where p, P, q and Q are orders of the various polynomials. Hence, the *seasonal ARIMA* process in (3) is said to be of order $(p,d,q)\times(P,D,Q)_s$.

Table 3.1 Logarithms of volume of retail sales

	Q1	Q2	Q3	Q4
1955	4.047	4.091	4.096	4.244
1956	4.060	4.111	4.133	4.278
1957	4.076	4.123	4.116	4.272
1958	4.074	4.130	4.124	4.300
1959	4.098	4.194	4.177	4.350
1960	4.156	4.234	4.220	4.381
1961	4.200	4.248	4.246	4.393
1962	4.196	4.257	4.260	4.402
1963	4.211	4.282	4.297	4.444
1964	4.258	4.309	4.315	4.472

2 The data is taken from Mills (1990: 169).

CHAPTER 4

FURTHER TOPICS IN TIME SERIES ANALYSIS

4.1 NON-STATIONARY TIME SERIES: INTRODUCTION

Usually macroeconomic time series show a tendency of growing over time and thus can be characterized as *trending*. This can be clearly seen in the real GDP performance, which is the primary indicator for tracking a domestic economy. However, if we were to take snapshots of an economy at different points in time, no two photos would look alike. The reason for this has concerned economists for some time. It appears that there exist seemingly random fluctuations around the growth trend. Indeed as Nelson wrote:

> An important fact about real GDP is that its growth rate is highly variable from quarter to quarter. The fact that real GDP may have increased rapidly last quarter clearly does not imply that the economy will continue to expand rapidly next quarter. In other words there is not much momentum in the economy from quarter to quarter. This "noisiness" in quarter-to-quarter growth suggests that a just-announced quarterly growth rate tell us little about the future direction of the economy.[1]

Moreover, there seems to be a connection between this phenomenon and the existence of the business cycles. Economists refer to this "noisiness" or movements about the trend as *business cycles* or *business fluctuations*. The existence of cyclical movements in macroeconomic data has always been an important issue in the business cycle research since Burns and Mitchell (1946) and different methodologies have been derived for its identification. One of the most popular approaches is to define the cyclical fluctuations as the difference from the trend line which is a deterministic function of time. The problem with time deterministic approach according to Zarnowitz and Ozyildirim (2001: 16–17) is that:

1 See Macroeconomics: An Introduction – Internet edition. Available at: http://www.econ.washington.edu/user/cnelson/macroeconomics.html

> … it is very unlikely that any given type of linear deterministic trend would persist over long stretches of time, surviving major structural and technological changes, wars, business expansions and contractions … From the point of view of cyclical analysis, the cost of using a linear trend is that the deviations from it contain indiscriminately all business-cycle, growth-cycle and shorter irregular movements combined. Thus, too much of the overall variation is attributed to business cycles. Moreover, the linear trends do a poor job of differentiating between good and bad economic times.

This chapter will review some fundamental contributions, based on the papers of Beveridge and Nelson (BN) (1981), Nelson and Plosser (NP) (1982), and Hodrick and Prescott (HP) (1980, 1997).

4.2 BEVERIDGE-NELSON (BN) DECOMPOSITION

The BN decomposition assumes that the data is non-seasonal, since "seasonal adjustment logically precedes business cycles analysis" (Beveridge and Nelson, 1981: 154). This starting with the analysis of a *non-stationary* class of ARIMA models, for which the first differences are a stationary process, i.e. it is necessary to define a series $w_t = y_t - y_{t-1}$.

From the properties of *Wold Decomposition* (see Appendix 3), the general ARMA process can be represented as:

$$w_t = \mu + \sum_{i=0}^{\infty} \lambda_i \varepsilon_{t-i}$$

where μ is the long run mean of the stationary process, $\lambda_0 = 1$ and ε_t is WN. The next step is to find the expectation of y_{t+k} which is given by:

(1) $E(y_{t+k} | \Omega_t) = \hat{y}_t(k) = y_t + E(w_{t+1} + \ldots w_{t+k} | \Omega_t) = y_t + \hat{w}_t(1) + \hat{w}_t(2) + \ldots$

Now, from *one-step ahead forecasts* as was previously shown (see Chapter 3), we find that: $\hat{w}_t(1) = \mu + \lambda_1 \varepsilon_t + \lambda_2 \varepsilon_{t-1} + \ldots$, which leads us to a more general case of *multi-step ahead forecasts*, that is given by:

(2) $\hat{w}_t(i) = \mu + \lambda_i \varepsilon_t + \lambda_{i+1} \varepsilon_{t-1} + \ldots$

Substituting (2) into (1) yields:

(3) $\hat{y}_t(k) = k\mu + y_t + \left(\sum_{i=1}^{k} \lambda_i \right) \varepsilon_t + \left(\sum_{i=2}^{k+1} \lambda_i \right) \varepsilon_{t-1} + \ldots$

Now, if we divide the right hand side of (3) into two parts, it can be seen that the forecast is of horizon k with *a slope equal to* μ and the *level* – also known as the *secular component or trend component* which is a stochastic process – is given by:

$$(4) \quad T_t = y_t + \left(\sum_{i=1}^{k} \lambda_i\right)\varepsilon_t + \left(\sum_{i=2}^{k+1} \lambda_i\right)\varepsilon_{t-1} + \ldots$$

It appears that the *level* is a random walk process with a drift. This is easily seen when computing the first differences and assuming an infinite forecast horizon, as follows:

$$T_t - T_{t-1} = y_t + \left(\sum_{i=1}^{\infty} \lambda_i\right)\varepsilon_t + \left(\sum_{i=2}^{\infty} \lambda_i\right)\varepsilon_{t-1} + \ldots - \left(y_{t-1} + \left(\sum_{i=1}^{\infty} \lambda_i\right)\varepsilon_{t-1} + \left(\sum_{i=2}^{\infty} \lambda_i\right)\varepsilon_{t-2} + \ldots\right) =$$

$$= w_t + \left(\sum_{i=1}^{\infty} \lambda_i\right)\varepsilon_t - (\lambda_1\varepsilon_{t-1} + \lambda_2\varepsilon_{t-2} + \ldots) = \mu + \left(\sum_{i=0}^{\infty} \lambda_i\right)\varepsilon_t$$

which straightforwardly results from the fact that:

$$w_t = \mu + \sum_{i=0}^{\infty} \lambda_i \varepsilon_{t-i}, \lambda_0 = 1$$

From (3) we already know that $\hat{y}_t(k) = y_t + \hat{w}_t(1) + \hat{w}_t(2) + \ldots = ku + T_t$, hence for infinite forecasting horizon that is, if $k \to \infty$, then we get the next equation:

$$(5) \quad T_t = y_t + \lim_{k\to\infty}\left\{\left[\hat{w}_t(1) + \hat{w}_t(2) + \ldots \hat{w}_t(k)\right] - ku\right\}$$

which can be interpreted as the current observed value y_t plus all forecastable future changes in the series beyond the mean rate of drift. Beveridge and Nelson regard the cyclical component of y_t as:

$$c_t = T_t - y_t = \lim_{k\to\infty}\left\{\left[\hat{w}_t(1) + \hat{w}_t(2) + \ldots \hat{w}_t(k)\right] - ku\right\} = \left(\sum_{i=1}^{\infty} \lambda_i\right)\varepsilon_t + \left(\sum_{i=2}^{\infty} \lambda_i\right)\varepsilon_{t-1} + \ldots$$

It is clearly the case that c_t is a *stationary* process in the case where w_t is a finite order of MA (Beveridge and Nelson, 1981).

To conclude, BN decomposition shows that any time series whose first differences are stationary can be decomposed into *a trend* that exhibits *random walk, with a rate of drift* and *stationary cyclical component*. In particular, once the trend is a stochastic one, then it is meaningful to think that the variation is due to trend and the cyclical component. Instead of representing the data as temporary fluctuations around a deterministic trend, this trend shifts as each new data point reveals new information about the future.

4.3 NELSON-PLOSSER (NP) APPROACH

The framework of NP analysis is based on investigating two classes of *non-stationary models*. The first class of such models consists of: (a) deterministic function of time, known as *time trend*; and (b) stationary stochastic process with zero mean. These models are called *trend-stationary processes* (TSP), and are more precisely given by:

$$(1) \quad y_t = \beta_0 + \beta_1 t + c_t$$

where c_t are the deviations from the trend which are given by the stationary and invertible ARMA process, such that $a_p(B)c_t = b_q(B)\varepsilon_t$; ε_t is WN.

The second class of models uses a differencing technique to render non-stationary time series stationary. Such models are called *difference-stationary processes* (DSP), and are given by:

$$(2) \quad \nabla y_t = \beta + d_t$$

where d_t is given by the stationary and invertible ARMA process, such that $a_p(B)d_t = b_q(B)\varepsilon_t$; ε_t is WN.

Now if we rewrite (2) and sum each equation then we obtain:[2]

$$(3) \quad y_t = y_0 + \beta t + \sum_{i=1}^{t} d_i$$

which implies that TSP and DSP are *superficially alike*, in particular being linear functions of time with some deviation from it. However, (1) and (3) are *fundamentally different* from each other for a number of reasons. First, the intercept

---

2
$$\left.\begin{array}{l} y_1 - y_0 = \beta + d_1 \\ y_2 - y_1 = \beta + d_2 \\ y_3 - y_2 = \beta + d_3 \\ \vdots \\ y_t - y_{t-1} = \beta + d_t \end{array}\right\} \Rightarrow y_t = y_0 + \beta t + \sum_{i=1}^{t} d_i$$

in (3) is not fixed but depends on historical data. In addition, the disturbances are *not stationary* but rather the variance and the auto-covariance depend on time. On the other hand (1) has a *fixed intercept* with *stationary disturbances*. Therefore, the forecast errors from the TSP process are bounded, no matter how long the forecast horizon we want to compute. Moreover, while the auto-correlations in disturbances can be exploited making short term forecasts, over long periods of time the only information we have is the mean of the process, that is $\hat{y}_t = \hat{\beta}_0 + \hat{\beta}_1 t$, *so that neither past nor current events have an influence on the forecast.* DSP, on the contrary, will have error variance that will increase without a bound, suggesting that the long term forecasts could be greatly influenced by *accumulation of past disturbances*.

Now, it is important to decide whether the time series is a member of TSP or DSP, *which is equivalent to asking if we should or should not difference the series.* For example, Box and Jenkins (1970), suggest checking the behavior of the auto-correlation function. In particular if the auto-correlations do not "die out" rapidly, then it might indicate that there is a root close to the boundary of the unit circle. In other words we have to treat the process as non-stationary in y_t and as stationary in ∇y_t or some higher difference. Pierce (1975) suggested a procedure based on the behavior of the auto-correlation of $\hat{u}_t = y_t - (\hat{\beta}_0 + \hat{\beta}_1 t)$ where $a_p(B)u_t = b_q(B)\varepsilon_t$; ε_t is WN and $\hat{\beta}_0, \hat{\beta}_1$ are OLS estimates of β_0, β_1.[3] Thus, if the behavior of $\hat{u}_t$ is found to be *non-stationary*, then y_t should be differenced. In that case, the linear deterministic trend is eliminated and this implies that we get a DSP. On the other hand, *stationary* behavior of $\hat{u}_t$ suggests that we should treat y_t as a TSP. Nevertheless, Nelson and Plosser (1982) used the unit root test proposed by Dickey and Fuller (1979) to determine whether the process is TSP or DSP. The simplest form of the model that was examined is given by a regression equation:

$y_t = \alpha + \rho y_{t-1} + \beta t + \varepsilon_t$ as $H_0 : \rho = 1, \beta = 0$ (for a further discussion see Nelson and Plosser, 1982: 143–5).

It must be noted that: (1) the *t-ratios* are not distributed according to what we know as the standard *t* statistic, but rather distributed with the Dickey-Fuller statistic denoted by τ. (2) Testing the hypothesis $H_0 : \rho = 1$ alone is sufficient given that the process with $\rho = 1, \beta \neq 0$ is excluded from consideration, since in such cases ∇y_t would follow a deterministic path ($\beta > 0$, or $\beta < 0$). For this reason higher order trends are also excluded.

---

3 Pierce (1975) suggested general models of the form:

$$y_t = \sum_{j=0}^{m} \beta_j t^j + \frac{b(B)}{\nabla^d a(b)} \varepsilon_t;\ m > d$$

For our purposes $m=1$ and $d=0$.

The testing procedure was conducted on several series of US macroeconomic data such as real GNP, industrial production, wages, unemployment rate, etc. The results in the overall impression showed an *existence of the unit root in the majority of the macroeconomic data*, that is most of the series should be classified as DSP processes where the notable exception is the *unemployment* rate. These results have important implications concerning modeling macroeconomic data. For example it is widely accepted to model the growth component as a deterministic trend, while the DSP suggests that this component is *non-stationary*. The variance in the TSP is attributed to the *cyclical component*, while DSP model allows attributing the variation to *both growth and cyclical components*. Nelson and Plosser conclude,

> Therefore, empirical analyses of business cycles based on residuals from fitted trends lines are likely to confound the two sources of variation, greatly overstating the magnitude and duration of the cyclical component and understating the importance of the growth component (1982: 160).

4.4 HODRICK-PRESCOTT (HP) FILTER

The HP filter is considered to be among the most favored empirical techniques of researchers who attempt to separate cyclical behavior from the long run path of economic time series, or more precisely, the aim of the filter is to remove *low frequency variation* from an economic time series data. The procedure was first introduced in working paper form in 1980, while well known it was published only 17 years later, in 1997.

Given the time series y_t in logarithms, the proposed filter is given by:

$$(**)\ HP = \underset{\{g_t\}_{t=-1}^{T}}{Min} \left\{ \sum_{t=1}^{T} (y_t - g_t)^2 + \lambda \sum_{t=1}^{T} [(g_t - g_{t-1}) - (g_{t-1} - g_{t-2})]^2 \right\}$$

where $c_t = y_t - g_t$ is the cyclical component. The filter also involves the parameter λ which is known also as the *smoothing parameter*, which penalizes the acceleration in the *growth-trend* component relative to the *cyclical component*. Simply put, if we look at the first term in the equation it *penalizes large residuals*, while the second part of the loss function *penalizes lack of smoothness in the trend*. It is widely acceptable that for quarterly data the researchers set $\lambda = 1600$, which originally Hodrick and Prescott explained as:

> Our prior view is that 5 percent cyclical component is moderately large, as is a one-eight of 1 percent change in the growth rate in the quarter. This led us to select $\sqrt{\lambda} = 5/(1/8) = 40$ or $\lambda = 1600$, as value for smoothing parameter (1997: 4).

Nonetheless, this parameter does not have an intuitive interpretation and its choice generated great discussion in time series analysis literature, especially when concerning the frequency of the data observed. For example, Dolado et al. (1993) and many others suggested $\lambda = 400$, as a result of dividing 1,600 by 4, which is the ratio of the number of observations per year by quarterly and annual data. In Eviews (popular econometric software), the default values of λ are 100, 1,600 and 14,400 for annual, quarterly and monthly data respectively.

Summarizing above, the HP filter solves the problem by allocating some weight to a linear time trend against the original data y_t. Therefore, if $\lambda \to 0$ then the trend component is becoming more of the data itself and the cyclical component is equal to zero. On the other hand, for large enough λ, $g_{t+1} - g_t$ tends to some constant β. In particular, for $\lambda \to \infty$, g_t approaches $g_t = g_0 + \beta t$, which implies that the solution of the optimization problem (**), presented above, is the least square fit of a linear time trend model.

4.5 DYNAMIC SYSTEMS: INTRODUCTION

Previous chapters illustrated an approach for examining and testing univariate time series by utilizing the BJ approach. However, a substantial part of macroeconomic analysis deals with long run equilibrium relationships determined by forces, such that "... equilibrium is a stationary point characterized by forces which tend to push the economy back toward equilibrium whenever it moves away" (Engle and Granger, 1987: 251). In particular, an important task of macro-economic research is testing hypotheses and estimating the relationships between the aggregate variables.

In the context of analyzing long run equilibrium relationships between different aggregate variables, econometricians developed and applied different models during the years. In this context we must mention *simultaneous equations models* which are based on *endogenous and exogenous* variables. This approach has been criticized on different grounds. For example, classification of the variables into endogenous and exogenous is sometimes problematic and arbitrary. The other reason is related to the forecasting problem of exogenous policy, which makes the models' parameters vary (Lucas, 1976).

The basic assumption in econometrics is that the variables should have a finite variance, which is obviously true if these variables are *stationary*. As a result, econometricians proceed *as if* stationarity can be achieved by removing *deterministic* components, such as time trends, etc. from the data. Following the previous idea, economists applied the BJ approach, which transformed non-stationary data by successive differencing before specification. However, differencing time series might cause difficulties in inferring long run relationships from the estimated model. Simply put, if the deviations from the equilibrium relationship affect future changes in a set of variables, then, estimating a differenced model may cause misspecification error.

It must be emphasized that econometric theory has its own dynamic time series methods, among which we can find, for example, *distributed lag* methods (infinite, finite, rational and geometric) (Greene, 2003); CO or PW algorithms for estimating time series regressions in the presence of autocorrelated errors and tests for detecting the presence of autocorrelations in the errors, such as DW and LM as was discussed in the literature survey.

Another issue that emerged in analyzing dynamic systems is known as the problem of *spurious regression.* This problem emerged in typical OLS analysis. Granger and Newbold (1974) showed that pairs of non-stationary time series could frequently display highly significant correlations *when there was no causal connection between them.* In other words, running a regression and finding a very high R^2 and a very low DW value, may indicate that the obtained results have no economic meaning.

In sections 4.6 and 4.7 we will review contributions related to modeling a dynamic system, that emanated from works of Granger (1969) and Engle and Granger (1987). It should be recalled that these works are important from a historical point of view, since the writers presented a change in the practical approach of econometric analysis. In particular, their works utilized the time series framework of BJ with the econometric analysis.

4.6 GRANGER CAUSALITY

The idea of causality is utilized not only in economics, but in many different fields such as physics, philosophy, etc. In economic analysis, our aim is to find a relation between variables. On the other hand, when we find correlation between two variables the immediate question which should be asked is *what is the reason for this correlation?* or *is there a reason at all?* For example, if we find correlation between salaries of teachers and use of cigarettes, does that really mean that raising salaries will increase the use of the cigarettes? Reasonable people would definitely argue with such a statistical correlation. But not all examples are so simple to judge. In a dynamic system, when several variables are considered simultaneously, the complicated cross-correlation patterns can arise from many possible models.

The above mentioned problem led Granger (1969) to develop a new technique, which exploits the interrelationships among multiple time series in a dynamic system. In the literature this is known as *Granger's Causality*. In this framework

Granger, premised that future cannot cause the present or the past. Thus, if event *A* occurs after event *B*, then *A* cannot cause *B*. At the same time, when *A* occurs before *B*, it does not necessarily mean that *A* causes *B*. This causal framework is not that which we logically assume in real life, but it is related to observing time series. For example, do movements in prices precede movements in the interest rate, or is it the opposite, or are the movements contemporaneous? For those reasons a new statistical test was developed, which is given by:

$$y_t = \sum_{i=1}^{k} a_i y_{t-i} + \sum_{i=1}^{k} b_i x_{t-i} + \varepsilon_t$$

where y_t and $x_t$are time series.

Then, series x_t fails to be the cause of series y_t in the sense of Granger's causality, if the regression estimates of $b_i = 0$, for all $i = 1, 2 \ldots k$.

Thus, we see that Granger's approach to the question whether x_t causes y_t, is determined by examining how y_t is affected by its past values (y's) and by adding the past values of x's. We must also mention that Granger's causality is more related to the word *precedence*, since all we are testing is whether a certain variable *precedes* another, and that we are not testing causality *as it is usually understood.*

4.7 COINTEGRATION AND THE ERROR CORRECTION MODEL (ECM)

As we already mentioned, an important issue in macroeconomic analysis is the ability to integrate short run dynamics with long run equilibrium. Short run changes in time series are frequently stationary, even when the time series themselves are non-stationary in the long run. Thus, the strategy of facing non-stationary data can be simple, that is, one might study only short run changes. However, economic theories are generally formulated for *levels* of the variables rather than for their *differences*. For example, theories of consumption examine the relationships between the levels of consumption, income and other variables, but not their growth rates. Engle and Granger realized that such a strategy discarded valuable information. Another example, which emphasizes the importance of analyzing non-stationary time series, is to consider that a randomly walking drunk has a faithful friend who follows him down the street from a safe distance to make sure he does not injure himself. Because he is following the drunk, the friend, viewed in isolation, also appears to follow a random walk, yet his path is not aimless, that is, it is largely predictable, conditional on knowing where the drunk is. Thus, not all long run associations between non-stationary time series are nonsense.

Cointegration

The ideas above led Granger (1981) to develop the *theory of cointegration*, which was later, elaborated in Engle and Granger (1987). In the framework of the theory, Granger defined the concept of *degree of integration of a variable.* A time series is said to be integrated of order d, if $(1-B)^d y_t$ is a stationary time series and denoted by $y_t \sim I(d)$. Thus, stationary variables are denoted by $I(0)$. Note that if $y_t \sim I(1)$ and $x_t \sim I(0)$ then $z_t = y_t + x_t \sim I(1)$, which implies that in a linear combination of the two variables, the variance of y_t dominates the variance of x_t.

Now, consider the linear equation $y_t = \beta x_t + z_t$. According to Granger this equation is meaningful in the sense that "... a simulation of the explanatory side should produce the major properties of the variable being explained" (1981: 121), that is, if for example, y_t is a seasonal time series, then seasonality is attributed also to x_t provided that ε_t is WN. Now, if we suppose that $y_t \sim I(1)$ and $x_t \sim I(1)$, then y_t and x_t are said to be *cointegrated* if $y_t - \beta x_t \sim I(0)$ and denoted as follows: y_t and x_t are $CI(1,1)$.[4] Therefore, we have to run a regression $y_t = \beta x_t + z_t$ and analyze whether $y_t - \beta x_t = z_t$ is either $I(0)$ or $I(1)$. The case with $I(0)$ indicates that y_t and x_t do not drift to far from each other, suggesting that there is a long run equilibrium relationship between the two time series. The disturbance ε_t might be interpreted as *disequilibrium error*, or the distance that the system is away from equilibrium at time t. Now, if z_t is $I(1)$, then there is no long run equilibrium existence, that is, regressing y_t and x_t, generates spurious relationships.

Error Correction Model

Although long run equilibrium can be estimated directly from $y_t = \beta x_t + z_t$, most of the time the system deviates from it. Therefore, it is also important to consider the short run relationships between the variables. The importance of cointegration in the modeling of non-stationary time series becomes clear in the *Granger's representation theorem*, which was first presented in Granger and Weiss (1983). There, it was shown that if y_t and x_t are $CI(1,1)$ for the following bivariate autoregressive system of order p:

$$x_t = \sum_{j=1}^{p} \gamma_{1j} x_{t-j} + \sum_{j=1}^{p} \delta_{1j} y_{t-j} + \varepsilon_{1t}$$

$$y_t = \sum_{j=1}^{p} \gamma_{2j} x_{t-j} + \sum_{j=1}^{p} \delta_{2j} y_{t-j} + \varepsilon_{2t}$$

4 The general case is given as follows: $y_t \sim I(d)$ (and $x_t \sim I(d)$, then y_t and x_t are $CI(d,b)$ if $y_t - \beta x_t \sim I(d-b)$ for $b > 0$.

then there must exist an *error* correction *model* (ECM) representation of the dynamic system presented above, of the following form:

$$\nabla x_t = \alpha_1(y_{t-1} - \beta x_{t-1}) + \sum_{j=1}^{p-1} \gamma_{1j}^* \nabla x_{t-j} + \sum_{j=1}^{p-1} \delta_{1j}^* \nabla y_{t-j} + \varepsilon_{1t}$$

$$\nabla y_t = \alpha_2(y_{t-1} - \beta x_{t-1}) + \sum_{j=1}^{p-1} \gamma_{2j}^* \nabla x_{t-j} + \sum_{j=1}^{p-1} \delta_{2j}^* \nabla y_{t-j} + \varepsilon_{2t}$$

The term $y_t - \beta x_t$ is zero if the system is in equilibrium and measures the extent to which the long run relationship is not satisfied. The coefficients α_1 and α_2 are interpreted as the speed at which y and x adjust to any discrepancy between them in the previous period. Thus $\alpha_i(y_t - \beta x_t)$ is the component that captures the long run effects, and the system is said to be in *error correction form*, that is, the characterized system of equations, has a built-in mechanism which enables adjustment towards equilibrium.

An important part of analysis for dynamic systems is testing for cointegration. It is suggested to apply the unit root test to check if y_t and x_t are both $I(1)$. The subsequent step is to regress y on x and check for the existence of a unit root on the estimated residuals $\hat{z}_t$. More specifically, the null hypothesis and the alternative in cointegration tests are:

H_0: z has a unit root or x and y are not cointegrated.

H_1: x and y are cointegrated.

It must be mentioned that new tests for unit roots have been suggested over the years. Among the popular tests are the approaches proposed by Said and Dickey (1984) known as the Augmented Dickey-Fuller (ADF) test and Phillips and Perron (1988) test. The null hypothesis in both of these approaches assume that a time series is $I(1)$ against the alternative that a time series is $I(0)$. In addition, a modified version of the ADF test is the DF-GLS test proposed by Elliot, Rothenberg and Stock (1996). On the other hand, testing for stationarity (i.e., the null hypothesis suggesting that y_t is $I(0)$), can be performed by the popular KPSS test proposed by Kwiatkowski, Phillips, Schmidt and Shin (1992) or via the Leybourne-McCabe test (1994).

Nevertheless, it seems that the cointegration and ADF procedures are successful in their own right. Moreover, cointegration theory is definitely the innovation in theoretical econometrics that has created great interest, as it combines both univariate and multivariate time series analysis.

CHAPTER 5

THE DEVELOPMENT OF SEASONAL ADJUSTMENT PROGRAMS

5.1 INTRODUCTION

Most economic data are subject to seasonal variation. The use of the term *seasonality* emanates from the fact that seasons exert an unquestionable influence on *economic activity*. In other words, it can be any effect that is stable in terms of timing, direction and magnitude over the years. These effects may be regular, yet they do show variation from year to year and are subject to changes in pattern over time. These changes are most commonly thought to evolve primarily in a stochastic rather than a deterministic way.

Different reasons cause seasonality. It might include *natural factors* like weather conditions, *administrative measures* such as beginning and ending dates of the school year, *cultural traditions* such as holidays, etc.

An important question that an economist should ask himself is *why should one undertake seasonal adjustment?* Seasonal adjustment produces data in which the values of neighboring months are usually easier to compare. Many data users prefer seasonally adjusted data because they want to see those characteristics that seasonal movements tend to mask, especially changes in the direction or trend of the series. Simply put, it helps with the *short term forecasting*, and helps determine the stages of the business cycle of the economy at a given time. Dagum wrote about the importance of seasonal adjustment in the following terms:

> Such knowledge provides the basis for decision making to control the level of the economic activity and it is of the upmost importance around turning points. For example, failure to recognize the downturn in the cycle (beginning of a recession) may lead to adoption of policies to curb expansion when, in fact, a recession is already under way. Therefore, the identification and estimation of the model followed by the seasonal variations must be made with a high degree of accuracy (1978: 1).

While economists, policy makers, and analysts, among others, understand the importance of seasonally adjusted data, users of seasonally adjusted data may not necessarily understand the methods by which such data is generated. Indeed, the computation and understanding of the algorithm of seasonally adjusted data can be a difficult task or even impossible task for professional statisticians, not to mention the statistically unsophisticated user. It appears that there is a conflict situation, such that users trust the seasonal adjustment procedure without necessarily understanding, in general, how seasonal adjustment procedure works. Moreover, what occurs when different procedures for seasonal adjusting data are available? This question can be attributed to many users of seasonally adjusted data, especially those who do not have enough knowledge regarding the tools utilized. Therefore, we will review the history of the development of seasonal adjustment programs. We begin with some historical facts regarding programs of interest.

5.2 A HISTORY OF SEASONAL ADJUSTMENT PROGRAMS

The initial software in seasonal adjustment was developed by the US Census Bureau in 1954, and was based on the *moving average* method. Its name was *Census Method 1*. In 1955 it was replaced by *Census Method 2*, resulting in version *X-3*. Over a decade *Census Method 2* underwent different developments, resulting in versions from *X-3* through *X-10*, culminating with the version known as *X-11*, in 1965. In 1975 Statistics Canada developed a program known as *X-11-ARIMA* which was based on both *X-11* and BJ approach (*ARIMA time series modeling*). This program was revised in 1988 and updated by a version known as *X-11-ARIMA/88*. The US Bureau of the Census then developed *X-12-ARIMA* (X-12) in 1998. The X-12 program is based on the Bureau's earlier X-11 program and the X-11-ARIMA program developed at Statistics Canada, and it is based on *RegARIMA* models (*regression models with ARIMA errors*). Interestingly enough, at about the same time Statistics Canada was augmenting the original X-11 program by combining it with the BJ approach, in the US, Bell Labs was developing what they called "SABL" (Seasonal Adjustment-Bell Laboratories) which they described as a "Resistant Seasonal Adjustment Procedure with Graphical Methods for Interpretation and Diagnosis" (Cleveland et al., 1978). However, this approach never became popular.

At present, the most popular seasonal adjustment method is the US Census Bureau's X-12 program. This program is widely used by central banks and statistical agencies around the world (for example, in US, UK, New Zealand and Israel, among other countries). In 2006, the US Census Bureau released a new version of the program, entitled the *X-13 ARIMA Signal Extraction in Time Series* (X-13-A-S). This version is different from the previous packages, since on the one hand it uses the seasonal adjustment based on MA filters, and the other hand it is based on *SEATS* (*Signal Extraction in ARIMA Time Series*) program of Gomez and Maravall (1996).

Another approach is the TRAMO/SEATS (*Time Series Regression with ARIMA Noise, Missing Observations and Outliers*) package, an approach of Gomez and Maravall (1996). This package performs signal extraction with filters derived from an ARIMA time series model that describes the behavior of the series. It utilizes the *ARIMA Model Based* (AMB) approach to signal extraction.

As noted, this chapter will review the historical development of adjustments programs. The main aim of these surveys is to emphasize the *methodological differences* between the different programs.

The discussion regarding X-11 procedure will be somewhat comprehensive, since it contains basic algorithms and features which were later revised in over time. We will also deal with X-11-ARIMA program, which represents the *fundamental change* in the concept of seasonal adjustment procedures. And finally, we will discuss two among the most popular programs for seasonal adjustment – the X-12 and TRAMO/SEATS programs.

5.3 X-11

In 1954, the US Bureau of the Census introduced Method 1 for seasonal adjustment via computer. The basic seasonal adjustment procedure *under the default option* of the Census Method decomposed time series data under a multiplicative model $Y_t = TC_t \times S_t \times I_t$, where: TC_t – trend cyclical component; S_t – seasonal component; I_t – irregular component. The decomposition was based on the *ratio to moving average* procedure described by Macaulay (1931).

The Census Method 1, was later upgraded in 1955 to Method 2, finally culminating in Method X-11 in 1965. The X-11 is based on the MA procedure, which will be now briefly discussed.

We will denote a simple MA by $M_{p\times q}$, where we have:

a) The weights are given by: $\dfrac{(1,...p-2, p-1, p, p...p-1, p-2...,1)}{p\times q}$

b) "p" appears as $|p-q|+1$ times in (a);

c) The order (number of terms) of the MA is $p+q-1$.[1]

For example:

$$M_{3\times5} \Rightarrow (1,2,3,3,3,2,1)/15 = (\tfrac{1}{15},\tfrac{2}{15},\tfrac{3}{15},\tfrac{3}{15},\tfrac{3}{15},\tfrac{2}{15},\tfrac{1}{15});$$

$$M_{2\times12} \Rightarrow (1,2,2,2,2,2,2,2,2,2,2,2,1)/24 = (\tfrac{1}{24},\tfrac{2}{24},\tfrac{2}{24},\tfrac{2}{24},\tfrac{2}{24},\tfrac{2}{24},\tfrac{2}{24},\tfrac{2}{24},\tfrac{2}{24},\tfrac{2}{24},\tfrac{2}{24},\tfrac{2}{24},\tfrac{1}{24})$$

The program also utilizes the *Henderson* MA. These filters are a widely used set of trend filters and will be denoted by $H_{p\times q}$.[2]

The Basic X-11 Algorithm: Method of Iteration for Monthly Data[3]

Seasonality in general cannot be identified until the trend is derived. On the other hand, an estimate of a trend cannot be made until the time series is seasonally adjusted. Therefore, the X-11 program decomposes the time series components via an iterative procedure. At each stage, the program judiciously utilizes pre-chosen albeit different MAs. Thus, the algorithm of X-11 can be divided into three main stages:

Stage 1

a) Compute a 13 term *symmetric* MA which is given by:

$$M_{2\times12}(Y_t) = TC_t^{(1)} = \frac{1}{24}Y_{t-6} + \frac{1}{12}Y_{t-5} + \dots \frac{1}{12}Y_{t+5} + \frac{1}{24}Y_{t+6}$$

which is also known as the *crude* estimate of a TC component.[4] The trend is then removed from the original series.

Remark – the notation $TC_t^{(1)}$ is referred to the trend-cycle component which was derived in the first stage. In general, the number in the brackets (right upper corner) is the *stage number*.

---

1 A $p \times q$ moving average is a p-term simple average taken over q consecutive sequential spans.

2 For different Henderson MA orders and the weights attributed to it, see for example "*An Introductory Course on Time Series Analysis-Electronic Delivery*", 2005, Information Paper, Australian Bureau of Statistics.

3 Note that analogous procedure can also be performed for a quarterly data.

4 For example, 2x12 trend filter for January 2006:

$$\frac{2005(7)}{24} + \frac{2005(8)+2005(9)+\dots 2006(1)+2006(2)}{12} + \dots \frac{2006(7)}{24}$$

b) Compute *SI-ratio*, which is given by:[5]

$$SI_t^{(1)} = \frac{Y_t}{TC_t^{(1)}}$$

c) Compute a 5 term MA, which is given by:

$$M_{3\times3}(SI_t^{(1)}) = S_t^{(1)} = \frac{1}{9}SI_{t-24} + \frac{2}{9}SI_{t-12} + \frac{3}{9}SI_t + \frac{2}{9}SI_{t+12} + \frac{1}{9}SI_{t+24}$$

It is then, an estimate of the *seasonally biased* component for each month.[6]

d) Compute the *seasonal unbiased* component

$$\tilde{S}_t^{(1)} = \frac{S_t^{(1)}}{M_{2\times12}(S_t^{(1)})}$$

where:

$$M_{2\times12}(S_t^{(1)}) = \frac{S_{t-6}^{(1)}}{24} + \frac{S_{t-5}^{(1)}}{12} + \ldots \frac{S_t^{(1)}}{12} + \ldots + \frac{S_{t+5}^{(1)}}{12} + \frac{S_{t+6}^{(1)}}{24}$$

e) Most time series contain *outliers* (extreme values). Such values can be caused by strikes, extreme weather conditions, war, etc. The X-11 program includes provisions to deal with such values, via means of statistical control principles. Each extreme value is analyzed, with respect to whether it is above or below a certain range (expressed in terms of standard deviations or multiples of *sigma*), and these extreme values can be modified or dropped before final estimates for seasonality are computed.

Hence, the program subtracts the estimate of the seasonal component from the SI-ratio given in (b), as follows:

$$I_t^{(1)} = \frac{SI_t^{(1)}}{\tilde{S}_t^{(1)}}$$

f) Compute the following, which is the initial *preliminary adjusted* time series:

$$A_t^{(1)} = \frac{Y_t}{\tilde{S}_t^{(1)}}$$

---

5 $SI_t = S_t \times I_t$

6 For example, 3x3 trend filter for January 2006:

$$\frac{1}{9}[2004(1)] + \frac{2}{9}[2005(1)] + \frac{3}{9}[2006(1)] + \frac{2}{9}[2007(1)] + \frac{1}{9}[2008(1)]$$

Up to now, the first stage of the decomposition of the time series has been presented. The result is a less seasonal time series, however the program continues in the iteration process to generate improved estimates of the time series components, as now will be seen.

Stage 2

a) Compute a Henderson MA on the initial seasonally adjusted time series from the first stage. The length of the Henderson filter is given by $2h+1$, and defined by the volatility of the data, or more precisely, it depends on the $\bar{I}/\bar{C}$ ratio (the ratio of the average absolute month-to-month change in the irregular to that in the TC component). Thus, for $0\,''\ \bar{I}/\bar{C}\,''\ 0.99$ use $h=4$; for $1\,''\ \bar{I}/\bar{C}\,''\ 3.49$ use $h=6$; for $3.49\,''\ \bar{I}/\bar{C}$ use $h=12$ (Shiskin et al., 1967).[7]

   Suppose that $h=12$, then we obtain a 13-term Henderson MA, such that the trend estimate is given by:

$$H_{13}(A_t^{(1)}) = TC_t^{(2)} = \sum_{j=1}^{13} w_j A_{t+j}^{(1)}$$

b) Compute the *SI ratio*, which is given by:

$$SI_t^{(2)} = \frac{Y_t}{TC_t^{(2)}}$$

c) Compute a 7 term MA, which is given by:

$$M_{3\times5}(SI_t^{(2)}) = S_t^{(2)} = \frac{1}{15}SI_{t-36} + \frac{2}{15}SI_{t-24} + \frac{3}{15}SI_{t-12} + \frac{3}{15}SI_t \frac{3}{15}SI_{t+12} \frac{2}{15}SI_{t+24} + \frac{1}{15}SI_{t+36}$$

   This is the *seasonally biased* component over each month.

d) Compute the *seasonal unbiased* component (the same procedure as in stage 1-(d)):

$$\tilde{S}_t^{(2)} = \frac{S_t^{(2)}}{M_{2\times12}(S_t^{(2)})}$$

   where:

$$M_{2\times12}(S_t^{(1)}) = \frac{S_{t-6}^{(1)}}{24} + \frac{S_{t-5}^{(1)}}{12} + \ldots \frac{S_t^{(1)}}{12} + \ldots + \frac{S_{t+5}^{(1)}}{12} + \frac{S_{t+6}^{(1)}}{24}$$

7 Higher volatility in the TS requires a longer MA.

e) Compute the following (the same procedure as in stage 1-(e)).

$$I_t^{(2)} = \frac{SI_t^{(2)}}{\tilde{S}_t^{(2)}}$$

f) Compute the following, which is the second stage preliminary adjusted time series.

$$A_t^{(2)} = \frac{Y_t}{\tilde{S}_t^{(2)}}$$

Stage 3

a) Compute the final TC component for a determined " h " that can be different from stage 2, which was initially 6:

$$H_{13}(A_t^{(2)}) = TC_t^{(3)} = \sum_j w_j A_{t+j}^{(2)}$$

b) Compute the final irregular factors as follows:

$$I_t^{(3)} = \frac{A_t^{(2)}}{TC_t^{(3)}}$$

Thus, the final estimated multiplicative decomposition is given as follows:

$$y_t = TC_t^{(3)} \times \tilde{S}_t^{(2)} \times I_t^{(3)}$$

We have shown the basic algorithm of X-11 program that is based on iterative procedure. The program could adjust the data with different kinds of MA without an underlying *explicit model* which was, mostly, a result of an empirical experience. The program also had an option to model the data in the *additive and log-additive forms* (Ladiray and Quenville, 2001).[8]

Other options provided by the program include:

Trading-day adjustment Different months have different numbers of days, and different numbers of trading-days. The *peak days* (high fluctuations that occur

8 By observing the plots of time series, it is possible to distinguish the characteristic difference between multiplicative and additive decompositions. In particular, in the additive case, the data shows *steady seasonal fluctuations, regardless of the overall level* of the series. In the multiplicative case, the size of the seasonal fluctuations varies *and depends on the overall level* of the series.

on such days) contribute significantly to the variability in a monthly objective variable. In general, trading day effects are estimated by assigning weights to each and every day of the week, that is, it is reflecting the level of activity in a specific day related to others. A regression framework can be applied to estimate the trading day effects from the original data (for a detailed discussion see Young, 1965). It should be noted that the trading day variation cannot be estimated when the time series exhibits high irregular variation. The X-11 variant allows the user to test whether such trading day variability exists in the series. Standard significance tests are applied in order to evaluate the reliability of the estimates (for a detailed discussion see Shiskin et al., 1967).

End point problem Since X-11 program utilizes symmetric filters, it can only be applied to regions of data that are sufficiently far away from the ends of the series. For example, a 13 term Henderson MA can only be applied to monthly data that is at least six observations from the start or end of the data. As we have already mentioned, the filters constructed for different spans of data were products of empirical research. Thus, assigning weights to the end data values had become an issue for a research. Shiskin et al. wrote:

> The end weights for the seasonal-factor and the trend-cycle moving-average curves are similar to those used in earlier versions of method 2. These weights assume that the future seasonal or trend-cycle values will be approximately the same level as the most recent values. While these weights give satisfactory results for most economic series, further research may yield end weights which are more suitable for series which have rapidly changing seasonal or cyclical patterns (1967: 4).[9]

The X-11-ARIMA method emerged from the necessity to rectify this weakness, as will be seen below in section 5.4 below. For a good survey of seasonal adjustment modeling considerations, see Hillmer, Bell and Tiao (1983).

5.4 SEASONAL ADJUSTMENT ISSUES

Moving Seasonality

This form of seasonality accounts for year to year variation in the seasonal component of a monthly and quarterly time series. For example, the increasing popularity in January (post-Christmas) sales has brought about both a change in monthly and quarterly retail sales data.

---

9 In the context of end point problem, moving average weights are discussed in appendix B at Shiskin et al. (1967).

Moving Holidays and Holiday Effects

Annual holidays whose exact timing shifts over the year affect economic activity and this must be taken into account in time series analysis and forecasting. Such holidays include, for example, religious holidays and New Year celebrations. These moving holidays can affect retail sales, tourism, stock market indices and other economic indicators. Holiday adjustment, therefore, is an integral part of both monthly and quarterly seasonal analysis. An example of holiday pre-adjustment in given in Chapter 6 (section 6.2).

Trading Day Effects and Adjustment

As is well known, the length of months in terms of number of weekdays varies from year to year. Each month is composed of four weeks and a few additional days. In other words, there are always four of each weekday, but in some months and years, some days will occur more often. Depending on which days these are, economic activity will be greater or less; this is especially important regarding retail sales and stock market activities.

Trading day effects can be estimated by assigning weights to days of the week reflecting the relative level of economic activity. Following from this, regression analysis is utilized to estimate the trading day effect for different days of the week, that is to say trading day daily weights, which are assumed to be constant over time. This however, may not reflect actual events and behavior, as regulations may change over time, such as trading hours, the stock market, or working hours and days in retail trading, resulting in moving trading day effects. For example, extension of sales hours or days in the retail sector over time will bring about moving trading day effects in both wholesale and retail sales. Length of month effects must also be considered in this context. In some cases, trading day and length of month effects do not strongly affect quarterly time series, in other cases they have to be taken into account, depending on the level of economic activity involved.

Outlier Adjustment

Extreme values, or outliers in time series can affect the trend depending on the extent of this activity, such that it is both necessary to identify and correct these irregular values. Strikes, wars, and "acts of God" (major climatic and geologic catastrophes) must be accounted for when analyzing time series, and their impact "smoothed" or totally removed, so as to minimize or eliminate their distorting effect on trend.

Breaks in Trend, Seasonal Breaks and Statistical Revision

Sustained changes for at least three successive quarters, or six months in the level of a time series, can be considered to be a break in trend. Shorter sustained changes are outliers, and should be treated as such. The reasons for a trend break can result from changes in policy, behavior, and measurement. For example, changes in tax policy, expenditure and savings patterns, or statistical definitions can bring about such breaks. Abrupt changes in seasonality can be considered seasonal breaks given that they do not affect the level of the series in question. These may result from various changes or innovations. Perhaps the most important structural break occurs with revision of components of a time series, and can encompass original data, seasonally adjusted data, and estimates of the trend. A significant example is the impact of data revisions on trend estimates of, and seasonally adjusted, unemployment data. A case study illustrating the issues above will be dealt with and discussed in Chapter 6.

Analysis and Adjustment

Forward factors and concurrent analysis The two approaches to determine trading day factors and analyze the possibility of changing seasonal patterns are forward factor and concurrent analysis. Annual analysis relates to the latest data available so as to determine trading day factors and the possibility of changes in seasonal factors for the upcoming year. The other method, concurrent analysis, is based on the re-estimation of trading day effects as new data are added to the series, in addition to the re-estimation of seasonal factors accordingly.

Method of Adjustment

Aggregative adjustment This method is based on the seasonal adjustment of the individual components of a time series, and then adding the results so as to generate the seasonally adjusted series. An example would be seasonally adjusting quarterly Consumption, Investment, and Government Expenditure series, then adding the results to obtain seasonally adjusted Gross Domestic Product.

Disaggregative adjustment This method is based on the summation of component series to generate the total series, and then directly seasonally adjusting the total series accordingly. Again, adding Consumption, Investment and Government Expenditure and then seasonally adjusting the total to obtain seasonally adjusted Gross Domestic Product would be an example of such a procedure.

The choice of adjustment method results from the structure of seasonal patterns in the time series comprising an overall series. If seasonal patterns vary widely between the components of an overall series, then the component series should be adjusted individually and added to generate the overall series.

5.5 X-11-ARIMA

The main criticism of the X-11 program concerned MA techniques, when the data point to seasonally adjust is at the extremity of the series of observations used to smooth the initial and final parts of the series. Following the BJ approach, the Statistics Canada, X-11-ARIMA program, was developed by Dagum in the 1970s. Later, it was modified to versions known as X-11-ARIMA/88. This technique consists primarily of adding raw data estimates for a certain year at the *beginning* and at the *end* of the initial series, before proceeding to the seasonal adjustment itself. In this section, we will introduce the main concepts of X-11-ARIMA procedure and outline the provision of the improvements relative to the X-11 program.

The general *multiplicative seasonal ARIMA model* is given as follows: $a_p(B)A_P(B^s)\nabla^d\nabla_s^D y_t = b_q(B)C_Q(B^s)\varepsilon_t$, where p, P, q and Q are orders of the various polynomials satisfying the stationarity and invertibility conditions (roots lie outside the unit circle). The *seasonal ARIMA model* is then given by a multiplicative representation as follows: $(p,d,q)\times(P,D,Q)_s$. In particular, the forecasts of the raw data are computed by the *multi-step ahead forecast* derived from the *MMSE forecast*. It must be noted that the MMSE forecasts are easily updated as new data becomes available.

Basic Properties of X-11-ARIMA

There is an option to construct an ARIMA model, or letting the program choose the appropriate one. The automatic selection of a model is based on empirical research over hundreds of time series, based upon both monthly and quarterly data. In particular, the ARIMA models to be automatically utilized must fit the data well, such that, generating forecast for the last three years, with mean absolute errors that are not higher than 5 percent for well-behaved data and 10 percent for more volatile data, respectively (Dagum, 1978).

The fact that ARIMA models are robust means that *identification can apply over several years*. This result is highly important, since it can avoid frequent changes of model and in particular, reduce the confusion between the users of seasonally adjusted data. Nonetheless, as more recent data is added, it is highly recommended to check the model identification of the time series, so as to ensure that the latest values follow the initial model.

The ability to increase the initial series for one or two years allows better analysis of the *end points* of the time series. It is well known that estimation of seasonal factors, both current and forecast, has a significant role, when seasonality is moving rapidly in a stochastic manner (this phenomenon happens in a large number of economic time series). Thus, the filters used in X-11 to seasonally adjust the data and to generate seasonal factors, are likely to use weights for *central observations*. As a result, the reliability of the extended series for current estimates is greater than that of the not extended series and the magnitude of revisions is significantly reduced.

The TC component is *no longer estimated with the end weights of a Henderson MA* (asymmetric weights), but with its *central weights*. This is the result of the extension of the initial time series through ARIMA forecasting procedures. Consequently, the Henderson MA *will not miss turning points when they occur at the ends of the initial data* (Dagum, 1978). Moreover, there is an option which allows for applying a *centered 24 term MA instead of centered 12 term MA* for the primarily TC component. As Dagum explained: "This new filter gives better results for series strongly affected by short cycles (less than three years) or sudden changes in trend" (1980: 8).

ARIMA Models and Extrapolation

We may ask the question: *How can we extend the initial series and what is an appropriate method to do this?* Different requirements are discussed in Dagum (1980). We must mention that the basic requirement is that the method for extrapolation to be chosen must belong to the *simplest class in terms of its description of the real world*. Simply put, the time series should be modeled by its *past values and lagged random disturbances, without the need for explanatory variables*. Moreover, if the extra values follow the behavior of the initial time series reasonably well (despite the fact that sometimes they can miss the level), *it reflects the fact that these values are not for policy or decision making, but rather to improve current seasonal adjustment.*

Advantages of X-11-ARIMA Over X-11 – Summary

The existence of a model is an important feature, since it means that the time series can be *extended* and therefore, be *decomposable*. In the case when the program does not fit an appropriate model (AR, MA, ARMA or ARIMA) the decomposition can be seriously criticized, in particular as the validity of the decomposed components is in doubt.

There are well-defined moments (expected value, variance) derived from ARIMA models. Thus, confidence intervals can be constructed for the observations, which is particularly important when analyzing the extreme values of the data.

The forecast procedure in X-11-ARIMA depends on model identification, which is unlike X-11, *where the procedures are the same for all time series*. This is *important* since the ARIMA filters are flexible, and two can better pick up the recent movements of the time series. In addition, for many time series, one revision alone can give seasonal factors that are final and significant.

The total error of seasonal factor forecasts has been reduced, in particular a reduction for example, of some 30 percent in the bias, and 20 percent in the absolute value, of the total error in Canadian and American time series. The set of weights applied to the irregular component allows a better estimation of its variance. Thus, it allows a better diagnostic of outliers, which as is well known, can severely distort the estimates obtained with linear smoothing filters. The X-11-ARIMA includes an improved diagnostic, different statistical tests and graphics (for detailed discussion see for example Dagum, 1980, 1999).

Based on the above for fitting and extrapolation, five ARIMA models were incorporated into the X-11 program in order to automate X-11-ARIMA. The user can define his model, or use automatic model selection. This procedure can be used for series that are at least five years long. For series of more than 15 years length, only the last 15 years should be used for diagnostics and extrapolating. The five models are tested sequentially in the following order: 1) if the model *i* is appropriate, then the program will stop diagnosing the other four models; 2) if the first step fails, then the program, will continue searching for a different model, and so on.

Automatic model selection chooses from the following ARIMA models:

* *Multiplicative and log additive decomposition*	* *Additive decomposition*
$\log(0,1,1)(0,1,1)_s$	$(0,1,1)(0,1,1)_s$
$\log(0,1,2)(0,1,1)_s$	$(0,1,2)(0,1,1)_s$
$\log(2,1,0)(0,1,1)_s$	$(2,1,0)(0,1,1)_s$
$\log(0,2,2)(0,1,1)$	$(0,2,2)(0,1,1)_s$
$\log(2,1,2)(0,1,1)_s$	$(2,1,2)(0,1,1)_s$

5.6 X-12-ARIMA (X-12)

X-12 is a seasonal adjustment program developed at the US Bureau of the Census. In general, X-12 includes all capabilities of X-11-ARIMA and X-11. The main change is an additional *pre-treatment for the data*, that is, it allows modeling either the *irregular series* or the initial one for *pre-adjustment*. It is based on a procedure called *regARIMA*, which helps to identify the *outliers*, *shifts of the level of time series*, *calendar effects*, and *estimation of seasonality at the start and end of the time series.*[10] These are *regression models with ARIMA errors*. In other words, in these models the *mean function of the time series* is described by a *linear combination of regressors*, and the *covariance structure of the series is that of an ARIMA process*. There are built-in regressors for directly estimating various trading day effects, holiday effects or sudden changes in level that have to be removed from the data before running the X-11-ARIMA and X-11 algorithm. Discussions about *trading day* regressors can be found in Young (1965), among other papers. *Calendar effect* variation discussed in Cleveland and Grupe (1983). Next we shall briefly describe the regARIMA procedure based on the paper of Findley, Monsell, Bell, Otto and Chen (1998).

General Model

It is sometimes suggested to stabilize the variance of the time series *before* estimating a RegARIMA model. Thus, a specified *non-linear transformation* of the data can be applied:

$$y_t^{(\lambda)} = f(Y_t) = \begin{Bmatrix} Y_t / d_t & \lambda = 1 \\ \lambda^2 + \left[(Y_t / d_t)^{\lambda} - 1 \right] / \lambda & \lambda \neq 0,1 \\ \log(Y_t / d_t) & \lambda = 0 \end{Bmatrix}$$

where Y_t is the original time series; d_t is an appropriate divisor (for detailed information about the devisors see at Findley et al., 1998: 31).

The pre-adjustment regression, i.e. RegARIMA model, is satisfied with values of $\lambda = 0,1$ and then the model becomes:

$$(*)\ a_p(B)A_P(B^s)\nabla^d \nabla_s{}^D (y_t - \sum_{i=1}^{r} \beta_i x_{it}) = b_q(B)C_Q(B^s)\varepsilon_t$$

where p, P, q and Q are orders of the various polynomials satisfying the stationarity and invertibility conditions (roots lie outside the unit circle).

The following term is a linear regression which has *time series of errors*, z_t.[11]

$$y_t - \sum_{i=1}^{r} \beta_i x_{it}$$

10 All these factors, as has already been discussed, can distort the seasonal adjustments.

11 When no regressors are used the RegARIMA model can be reduced to ARIMA model.

The latter time series is assumed to follow an ARIMA process. According to econometric theory, it is well known that errors based on the linear regression ought to be *uncorrelated* over time. On the other hand, for time series data in general, the errors can produce an *autocorrelation* and thus can be differenced. It follows then:

$$(**)\ w_t = \nabla^d \nabla_s{}^D \sum_{i=1}^{r} (y_t - \beta_i x_{it})$$

is a covariance stationary series that satisfies:

$$a_p(B) A_P(B^s) w_t = b_q(B) C_Q(B^s) \varepsilon_t$$

In addition, model given in (*) can be rewritten as:

$$\nabla^d \nabla_s{}^D y_t = \sum_{i=1}^{r} \beta_i \left\{ \nabla^d \nabla_s{}^D x_{it} \right\} + w_t$$

We have shown the regression model for a differenced y_t with stationary ARMA errors is given by w_t. Since ε_t is WN, then all parameters can be computed by maximizing the *likelihood function*.

Identification of the ARIMA Part of the Model

The automatic ARIMA modeling procedure is based on X-11-ARIMA, with five models that were previously discussed. If no regression variables are included, then a pure ARIMA procedure is obtained, which relies upon standard examinations of sample autocorrelations and partial autocorrelations. Nonetheless, the user can specify an alternative set of models for consideration. Thus, the fit of a model is decided on the basis of different tests such as Box-Ljung (Ljung and Box, 1978), Akaike Information Criterion (AIC) (Akaike, 1973) and Bayesian Information Criterion (BIC) (Schwartz, 1978), etc.

Beside the fundamental change of utilizing regression models with ARIMA errors, the program implements several new tools, like the *spectrum* of the different type of components, *sliding spans diagnostics* (see for example Findley et al., 1990).

5.7 TRAMO/SEATS

TRAMO

This is a program for estimation and forecasting of regression models with non-stationary (ARIMA) errors and a sequence of missing values in the series. The program interpolates these values and in addition it corrects the different types of outliers. It also estimates effects such as *trading day*, *leap year* and *non-stationary holiday effect* (e.g. Easter).

The general model of TRAMO is as follows:

$$y_t = \sum_{i=1}^{r} \beta_i x_{it} + v_t$$

where

$$\phi(B)\delta(B)v_t = \theta(B)\varepsilon_t$$

such that:

$$\delta(B) = \nabla^d \nabla_s^D;\ \phi(B) = (1+\phi_1 B + ... + \phi_p B^p)(1+\Phi_1 B^s + ... + \Phi_P B^{s\times P})$$

$$\theta(B) = (1+\theta_1 B + ... + \theta_q B^q)(1+\Theta_1 B^s + ... + \Theta_Q B^{s\times Q});\ \varepsilon_t \sim WN(0,\sigma^2)$$

The first term of the right hand side of the regression model is the effect which has to be removed, so the original series could be transformed into a series that can be assumed to follow ARIMA model. These regression variables can be *input by the user or generated by the program*. For example, variables that can be generated by the program are trading day, Easter effect etc.

SEATS

This is a program for estimation of unobserved components in time series which is based on the AMB approach. The program first identifies an ARIMA model for an *observed series*, and then decomposes the unobserved components. SEATS uses *signal extraction* technique. The optimal filter is derived from a time series model of the ARIMA-type which describes the behavior of the series while the components are explicitly specified (Planas, 1998). This method is based on works of Burman (1980), Hillmer and Tiao (1982) among other papers. In general, after TRAMO fitted the regression model

$$y_t = \sum_{i=1}^{r} \beta_i x_{it} + v_t$$

and we obtained an ARIMA model for v_t, i.e. $\phi(B)\delta(B)v_t = \theta(B)\varepsilon_t$, SEATS decomposes v_t in the following form:

$v_t = p_t + u_t + s_t = n_t + s_t$, where p_t, u_t, s_t are trend-cycle, irregular and seasonal components that *also follow ARIMA-type models*, and n_t is the seasonally adjusted series.

These programs, TRAMO and SEATS, then, decompose the components by utilizing *different techniques and tests* which are described in Gomez and Maravall (1997), Caporello and Maravall (2004). For implementation of TRAMO/SEATS, as Gomez and Maravall observe:

> Although TRAMO can obviously be used by itself, for example, as a forecasting program, it can also be seen as a program that polishes a contaminated "ARIMA series". That is, for a given time series, it interpolates missing observations, identifies outliers and removes their effect, estimates Trading Day and Holiday Effect, etc., and eventually produces a linear purely stochastic process. Thus, TRAMO, can be viewed as a pre-adjustment process to SEATS… (1997: 5).

Moreover, according to Caporello and Maravall:

> The two programs are structured so as to be used together both for in-depth analysis of a few series … or for automatic routine applications to a large number of series … (2004: 9).

CHAPTER 6

EMPIRICAL ANALYSIS

6.1 INTRODUCTION

In this monograph we have reviewed different approaches and techniques utilized in time series analysis. The following empirical examples and case studies will demonstrate: (a) different capabilities of seasonal adjustment programs i.e. X-12-ARIMA and TRAMO/SEATS, and how to utilize these programs in the best possible manner; (b) possible approaches to *forecasting*, estimating *and* testing the relationships between macroeconomic time series such as *Cointegration* and *Granger Causality*. These examples and case studies, in particular, will show the *synthesis* between econometric and time series analysis that has occurred over the past four decades, since the sea-change after the work of Box and Jenkins, and Granger and Newbold, among others.

6.2 SEASONAL ADJUSTMENT PROGRAMS AND AUTOMATIC PROCEDURES – EXAMPLES

In the analysis below we show the capabilities of the seasonal adjustment programs discussed. The approach of this analysis is simple and intuitive. Its aim is not to show whether one program is *better* than another, but rather to help the user in understanding the overall picture when dealing with adjustment programs and utilize them with *judgment*.

Three time series were chosen as examples so as to illustrate the outcome of automatic procedures and issues related to them:

1. *Israeli Electricity Consumption Data.*
2. *Israeli Tourism Data.*
3. *US Retail Sales Data.*

These three time series are special in the sense that they display highly seasonal fluctuations. These time series are filtered by X-12-ARIMA and TRAMO/SEATS respectively. In particular, seasonally adjusted data and TC components are compared.

Example One[1]

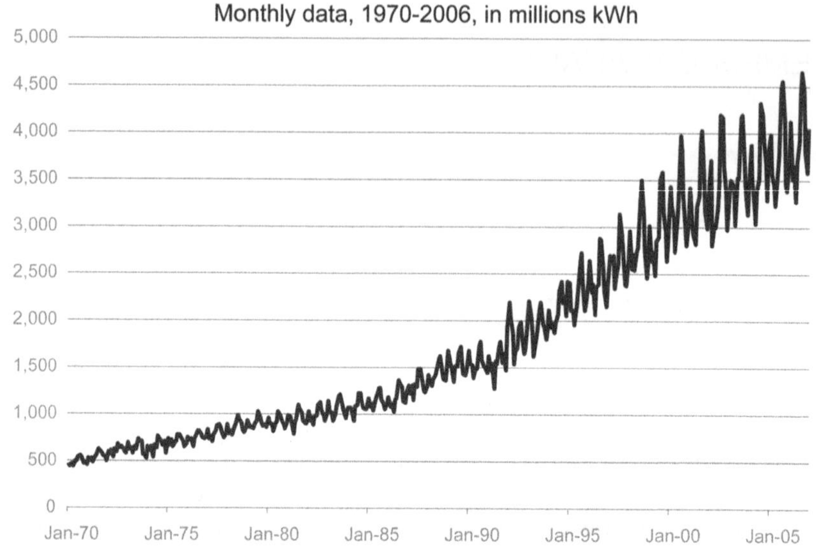

Figure 6.1 Electricity consumption in Israel, monthly data

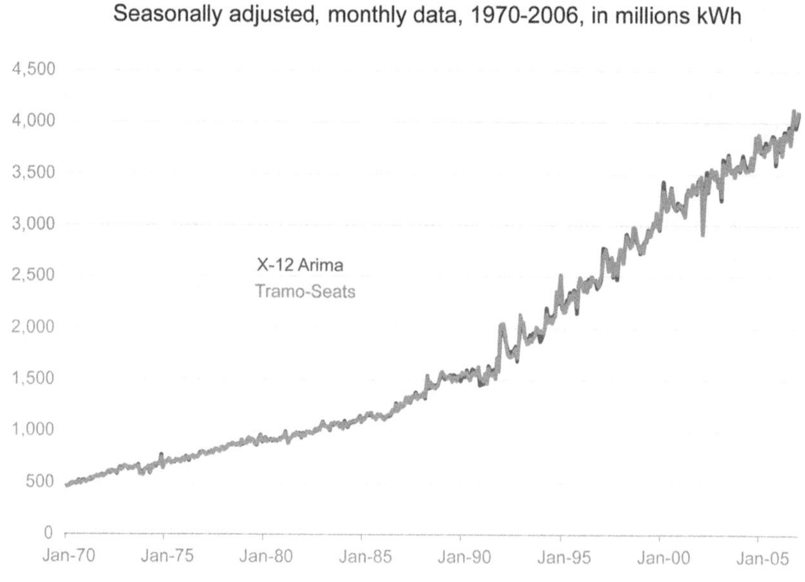

Figure 6.2 Electricity consumption in Israel, seasonally adjusted

---

1 Data source: Central Bureau of Statistics (Israel).

From the practical point of view, the figure above of the seasonally adjusted data, shows that in the *long run*, the automatic procedures produce "*quite*" *identical* results regarding *this* specific data set. In the figures below we observe the *decomposed* TC component. In this example, the difference between the computed TC components becomes clearer over the *short period*, 1990–1994, as can be seen in the latter figure. A closer investigation of short periods of time is therefore *highly recommended.*

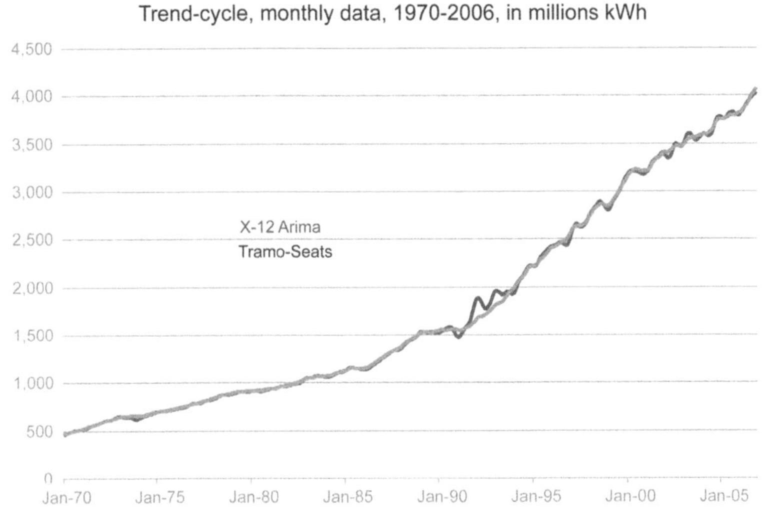

Figure 6.3 Electricity consumption in Israel, trend-cycle

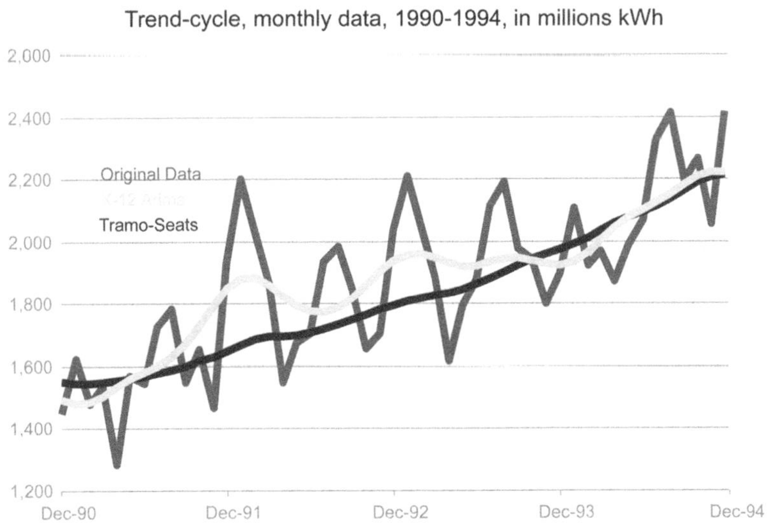

Figure 6.4 Electricity consumption in Israel, trend-cycle monthly data

Example Two[2]

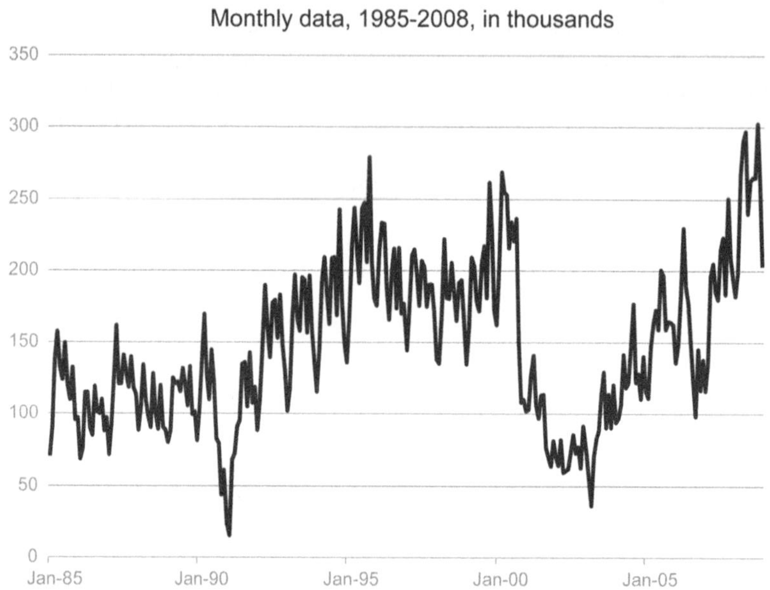

Figure 6.5 Tourist arrivals in Israel, in thousands

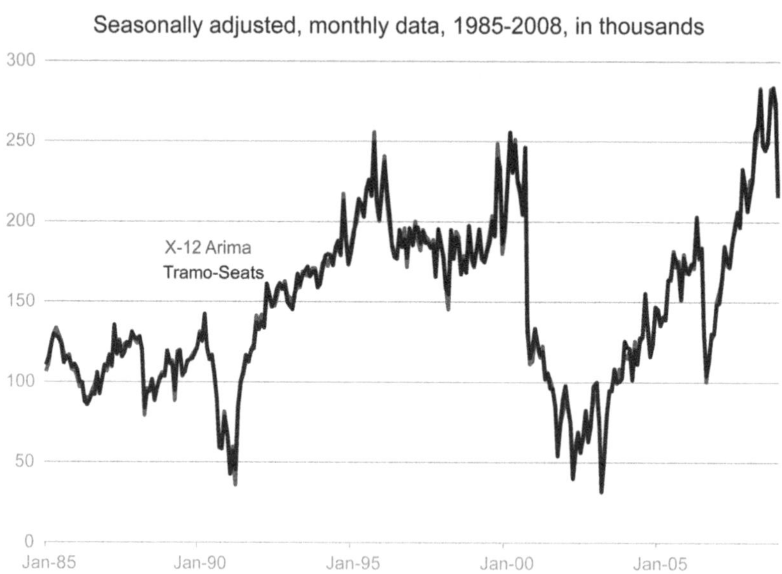

Figure 6.6 Tourist arrivals in Israel, seasonally adjusted

2 Data source: Bank of Israel.

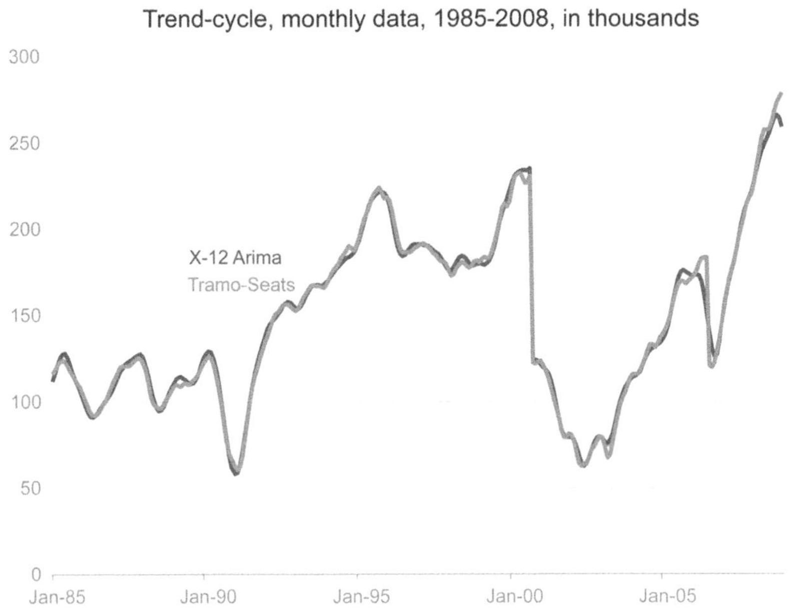

Figure 6.7 Tourist arrivals in Israel, trend-cycle

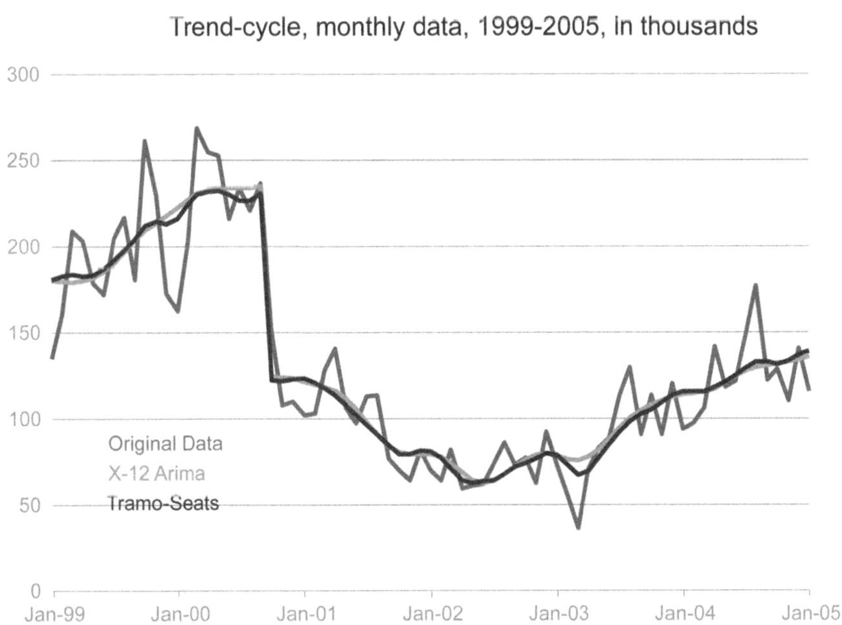

Figure 6.8 Tourist arrivals in Israel, trend-cycle monthly data

Example Three[3]

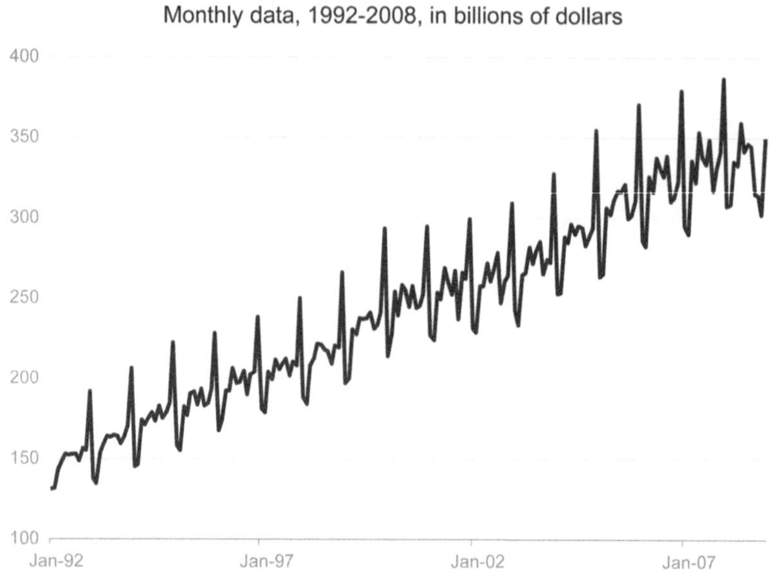

Figure 6.9 Retail sales in United States, monthly data

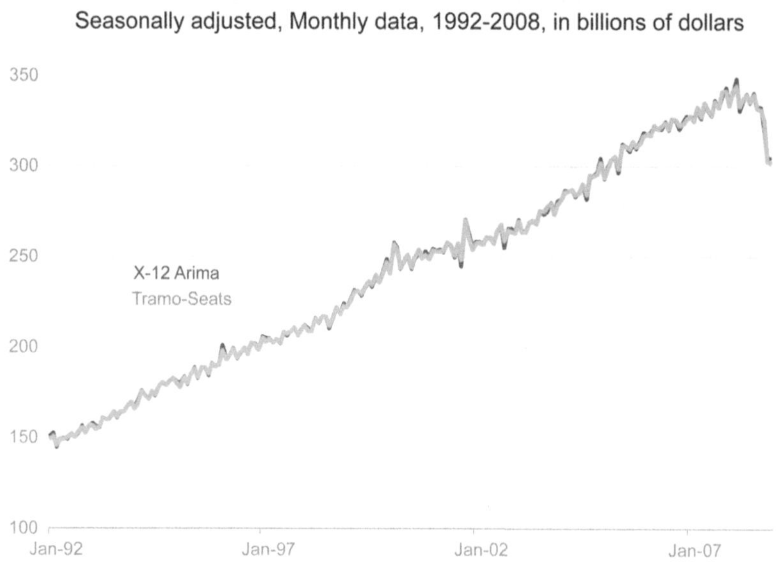

Figure 6.10 Retail sales in United States, seasonally adjusted

3 Data source: Economagic.com

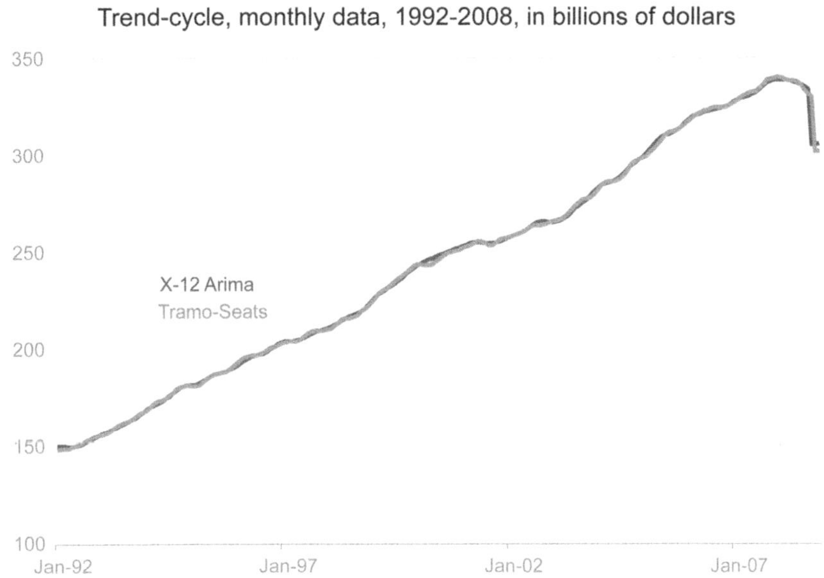

Figure 6.11 Retail sales in United States, trend-cycle

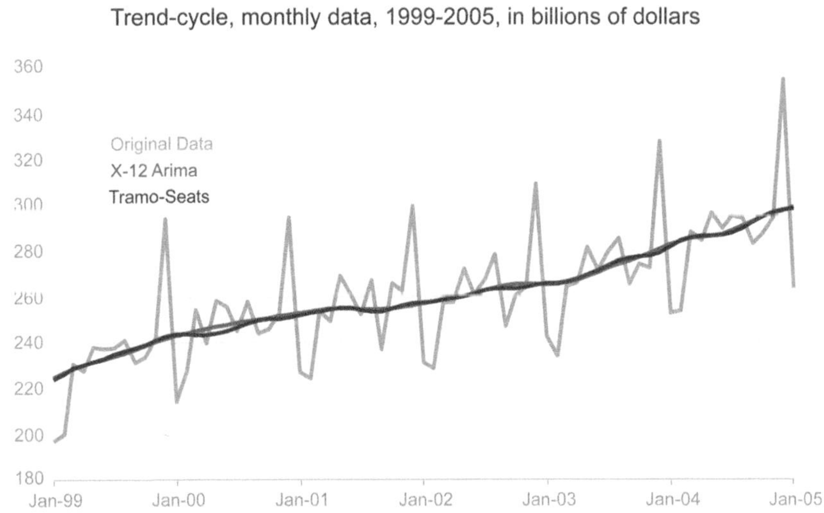

Figure 6.12 Retail sales in United States, trend-cycle monthly data

Example Two also shows distinct differences in TC component between the two adjustment methods over the short period 1999–2005 and afterwards; and differences in TC component can also be observed over short periods in Example Three, Figure 6.12. Detailed scrutiny of these three examples makes the overall picture clearer. In particular, when one is looking for *new information* that a time series can provide, for example, *changes* in trends and its impact for business cycles, the results of the two software programs show *differences over short periods of time. Therefore, a closer investigation of short periods of time is recommended so as to obtain a better overall picture of the process.*

It should be recalled, however, that many macroeconomic analyses rely on the fact that the data *has already been seasonally adjusted.*[4] Such results could be sufficient for further analysis, since the superiority, or otherwise, of one seasonal adjustment procedure over another is not the *prime concern* of these types of analyses. For example, further analysis that is based on seasonally adjusted data can be utilized by applying Hodrick-Prescott (HP) filter, as shown in the figure below (based on *Israeli Electricity Consumption Data*).

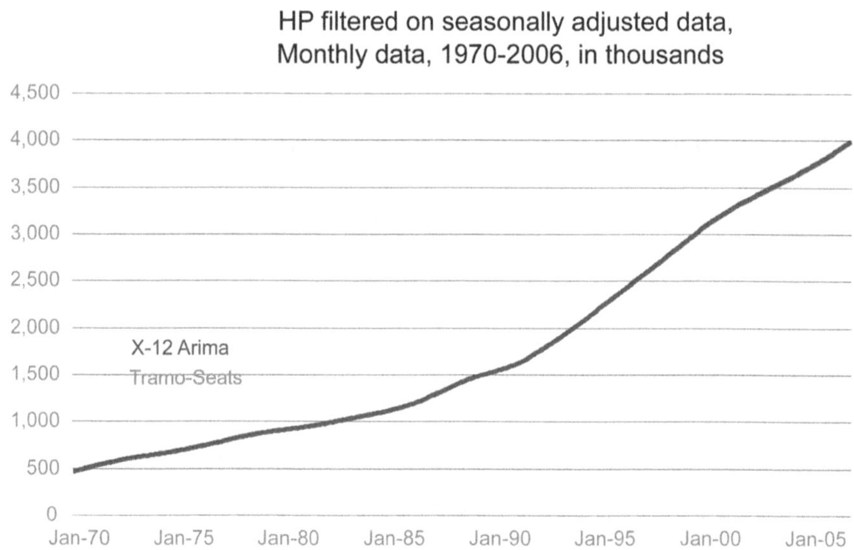

Figure 6.13 Electricity consumption in Israel, monthly data

In the figure above, the HP filter smoothes the seasonally adjusted data from both packages. It can be seen that in *this* specific data set there is no significant difference between the trends.

4 "Actually, there is also a seasonal component, but as the data are seasonally adjusted, this component has already been removed by those preparing the data series" (Hodrick and Prescott, 1997: 3).

6.3 HOLIDAYS EFFECTS: AN EXAMPLE OF PRE-ADJUSTMENT

In brief, the holiday effects adjustment procedure was, before *automatic* adjustment, composed of three stages. First, the raw data was fed into the X-11 program and a series of irregular factors generated accordingly (these included unusual events, calendar effects, and stochastic noise). A regression of the form outlined below was then run:

$$I_{ij} = \alpha + \beta W_{ij} + F_{ij} + \varepsilon_{ij}$$

for each calendar month j, $j = 1 \ldots\ldots 12$, and where:

F_{ij} = The date of the holiday in the year I measured as the number of days the actual holiday date in the respective year falls later than the earliest possible holiday date.

W_{ij} = The number of working days in month j of year i.

ε_{ij} = Stochastic elements.

The number of observations for each equation is set according to the number of years for which data is available. The non-significant variable is then removed from the regression, and the final form estimated (thus the equation for the month of June, for example, will not include the holiday variable F as an explanatory variable, and it will not be included a priori, so that any adjustment regarding June refers to working days, i.e. the length of the month, rather than holiday effect). Occasionally, the regression equation would not include the constant term α for, due for the most part to its multicollinearity with W, which is of low relative variance.

As output from the reduced form model we would obtain the forecast irregular factors, which were then applied as adjustment factors to correct for holiday dates varying between months or a varying number of workdays, in the case of this form of adjustment, where the forecast irregular factor was that part of the regularity which could be explained by the variables F and W. The original series was then divided by the forecast irregular factors, and pre-adjusted (that is to say pre-filtered) accordingly. The X-11 program was then rerun on the adjusted data. In today's augmented seasonal adjustment programs these procedures are done automatically, however the time series analyst should be aware of what these automatic procedures actually do.

6.4 BOX-JENKINS FORECASTING: AN EXAMPLE USING QUARTERLY DATA

Here we give an example of the Box-Jenkins technique as applied to a specific problem in short term forecasting. This series we took as an example was the number of hire-purchase contracts for new automobiles in England and Wales from 1958–69 (quarterly). Allard, in his study of hire-purchase made while at the British Treasury, found that the principle variables that explain movements in this series – which gave a general impression of the effects of government policy on the credit purchase of consumer durables –were as follows:

a) personal disposable income;
b) companys' trading profits;
c) the rate of purchase tax; and
d) a composite variable based on the rate of interest on hire-purchase contracts, the maximum repayment period, and the minimum deposit rate (Allard, 1974, 1975).

Later we consider ex-ante, post-sample forecasts using Allard's data generated by the Box-Jenkins techniques for the period in question. But first let us look at the results of applying the Box-Jenkins method to the series itself. The autocorrelations and partial autocorrelations of the original series (X_t), in addition to regularly differenced, seasonally differenced, and a combination of these two types, i.e. $(1\text{-}B)\,X_t$, $(1\text{-}B^4)\,X_t$, and $(1\text{-}B)\,(1\text{-}B^4)\,X_t$, are given in the following tables:

Table 6.1 Original series (X_t)

Lag-*k*	r_k	Φ_{kk}	Lag-*k*	r_k	Φ_{kk}
1	.67	.67	11	.16	.04
2	.37	–.14	12	.25	–.03
3	.46	.51	13	.08	.00
4	.63	.24	14	–.06	–.04
5	.38	–.40	15	.05	–.04
6	.17	.14	16	.09	–.08
7	.31	.15	17	–.07	–.05
8	.42	–.11	18	–.21	–.12
9	.21	–.06	19	–.16	–.14
10	.03	–.04	20	–.14	–.06

Note: Mean = 58.6 / Variance = 499.9

Table 6.2 Regularly differenced series (1-*B*) X_t

Lag-*k*	r_k	Φ_{kk}	Lag-*k*	r_k	Φ_{kk}
1	–.04	–.04	11	.02	–.13
2	–.65	–.66	12	.43	–.09
3	–.10	–.31	13	–.01	.03
4	.67	.34	14	–.41	–.09
5	–.08	–.30	15	.04	.00
6	–.57	–.22	16	.34	–.06
7	.04	.08	17	–.00	.00
8	.57	–.03	18	–.32	.04
9	–.05	.02	19	.03	.01
10	–.52	–.03	20	.25	–.03

Note: Mean = 0.9 / Variance= 318.1

Table 6.3 Seasonally differenced series (1-B^4) X_t

Lag-*k*	r_k	Φ_{kk}	Lag-*k*	r_k	Φ_{kk}
1	.65	.65	11	–.11	–.09
2	.18	–.41	12	–.08	–.11
3	–.17	–.14	13	.00	.08
4	–.30	–.04	14	.05	–.02
5	–.21	.10	15	.08	.07
6	–.04	–.01	16	.08	–.07
7	.06	–.05	17	.08	.08
8	–.02	–.22	18	.08	.03
9	–.12	.04	19	.06	.03
10	–.13	.03	20	–.02	–.18

Note: Mean = 3.3 / Variance= 313.9

Table 6.4 Combined differenced series (1-*B*) (1-B^4) X_t

Lag-k	r_k	Φ_{kk}	Lag-k	r_k	Φ_{kk}
1	.15	.15	11	–.01	–.02
2	–.16	–.19	12	–.06	–.21
3	–.31	–.26	13	.04	–.10
4	–.33	–.31	14	.02	–.18
5	–.08	–.14	15	.05	–.02
6	.10	–.10	16	–.02	–.16
7	.27	.06	17	.01	–.12
8	.00	–.22	18	.03	–.10
9	–.12	–.16	19	.09	.12
10	–.05	–.03	20	.00	–.09

Note: Mean = –0.2 / Variance= 224.5

We can draw a number of conclusions from the results as presented above:

The autocorrelations of X_t, the original series, do not damp out, and thus we must difference the series.

The autocorrelations of the regularly differenced series, (1-*B*) X_t, do not damp out for multiples of k =4, meaning that some form of seasonal differencing is, therefore, required.

The autocorrelations of the regular seasonally differenced series are adequate for model building, since those of the combined differenced series indicate "over filtering". However, following the principle of "over-fitting", we also use this form (Nelson, 1973: 114).

In addition, the results suggest that a mixed autoregressive seasonal moving average model of the form ARIMA (2, 0, 0) $(0, 1, 1)_s$ can readily be applied, since, Table 6.3, the autocorrelations die out by $k = 2$, and the "kink" at $k = 4$ would be removed by the seasonal moving average filter. One model we fit, therefore, is of the form:

$$(1-\varphi_1 B- \varphi_2 B^2)(1-B^4) X_t = (1-\theta B^4)\, a_t$$

The equation's parameters were estimated by a non-linear regression technique, and resulted in the following estimates, with standard embers of estimate in parentheses: estimates of $\varphi_1 = 0.92$ (0.17), $\varphi_2 = -0.37$(0.19), and $\theta = 0.21$(0.21).

The error variance as estimated (158.0) represents a decrease of 68 percent in the variance of X_t. The autocorrelations of the residuals are shown in Table 6.5:

Table 6.5 Autocorrelations of residuals $r_k(\hat{a})$

Lag-*k*	$r_k(\hat{a})$	Lag-*k*	$r_k(\hat{a})$
1	–0.02	11	–0.01
2	–0.04	12	–0.16
3	–0.01	13	0.00
4	–0.02	14	–0.02
5	–0.11	15	0.05
6	–0.04	16	–0.07
7	0.18	17	–0,01
8	–0.03	18	0.00
9	–0.13	19	0.04
10	–0.04	20	–0.06

However, four of the original 46 data points are "lost" by using the difference filter $(1\text{-}B^4)$, thus resulting in 42 "effective" observations in the sample. Now the Q statistic in our case has the following value: Q = 4.49. This test statistic, when compared to the tabulated value of χ^2 for 17 degrees of freedom, proved to be less than this value at a significance level of 99 percent. This confirms that there doesn't exist any evidence of significant departure from "white noise" i.e. randomness, as regards the era series, which come in this case, is the residuals, as noted.

But, as indicated previously, the preliminary analysis also suggests a very model specification. This is of the form ARIMA $(0,1,1)(0,1,1)_s$, since the autocorrelations in Table 6.4 die out by k= 1, and the partials marshals as a "sine-wave", so that the kink around $k = 4$ would be removed by seasonal moving average filter, given that we are using the combined regularly and seasonally differenced filter $(1\text{-}B)(1\text{-}B^4)$. In this case the model is of the form:

$$(1\text{-}B)(1\text{-}B^4)\,X_t = (1\text{-}\theta_1 B)\,(1\text{-}\theta_2 B^4)\,a_t$$

and the estimated parameters were as follows:

estimate of $\theta_1 = 0.01\ (0.16)$

and $\theta_2 = 0.56(0.15)$.

In addition, the error variance was equal to 195.1, a good deal more than that of the first alternative. Thus, the combination of high variance and insignificance in parametric estimation for one of the two moving average terms leads us to reject this specification and choose the first alternative, i.e. ARIMA (2,0,0) $(0,1,1)_s$ as preferable for forecasting purposes. An inspection of the autocorrelations shown in Table 6.5 does not suggest any alternative specification, so we used ARIMA (2, 0, 0) $(0, 1, 1)_s$, to generate forecasts accordingly. The results of the comparison between Box-Jenkins-based and the econometric based-forecasts generated by Allard (1974, 1975) appeared in Young (1977), and showed that the Box-Jenkins forecasts were better than Allard's own for the forecast periods be considered.

6.5 FORECASTING, COINTEGRATION AND GRANGER CAUSALITY: POSSIBLE APPROACHES AND CASE STUDIES

Case Study 1: Time Series Models and Forecasting of Electricity Consumption in Israel

We start by observing the original data. In general, many economic time series require *logarithmic* transformation before first differencing. We follow this procedure in our analysis.

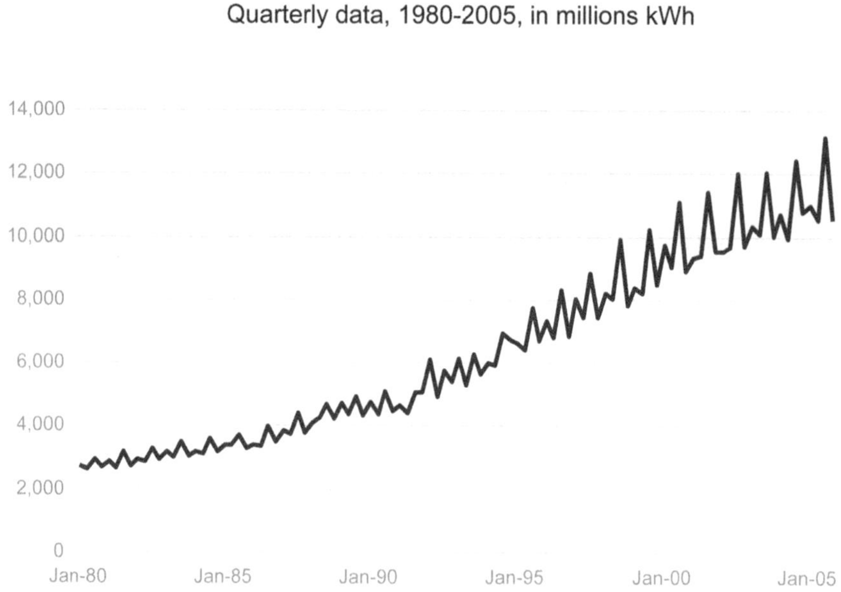

Figure 6.14 Electricity consumption in Israel, quarterly data

From inspection of the figure opposite, it can be ascertained that the original time series is not stationary, that is, differencing is necessary. Following the BJ approach, further inspection of the autocorrelations and partial autocorrelations gives us a clue regarding possible time series models that could properly represent the data. First, we examine the correlogram of the *seasonally differenced* data. As it can be seen in the figure below, the behavior of the autocorrelations and partial autocorrelations suggests that: (a) the series is stationary after only seasonal differencing; and (b) the process tends to be described by moving average models.

Thus, three reasonable models were chosen for examination as follows:

1. (0,0,1)*(0,1,0).
2. (0,0,1)*(0,1,1).
3. *Seasonal* (0,1,1).

These models can be described by the general seasonal ARIMA model of the form $a_p(B)A_P(B^s)\nabla^d\nabla_s^D y_t = b_q(B)C_Q(B^s)\varepsilon_t$, where p, P, q and Q are orders of the various polynomials. We continue with the estimation results for the different models, and the forecasts are computed for one year ahead.

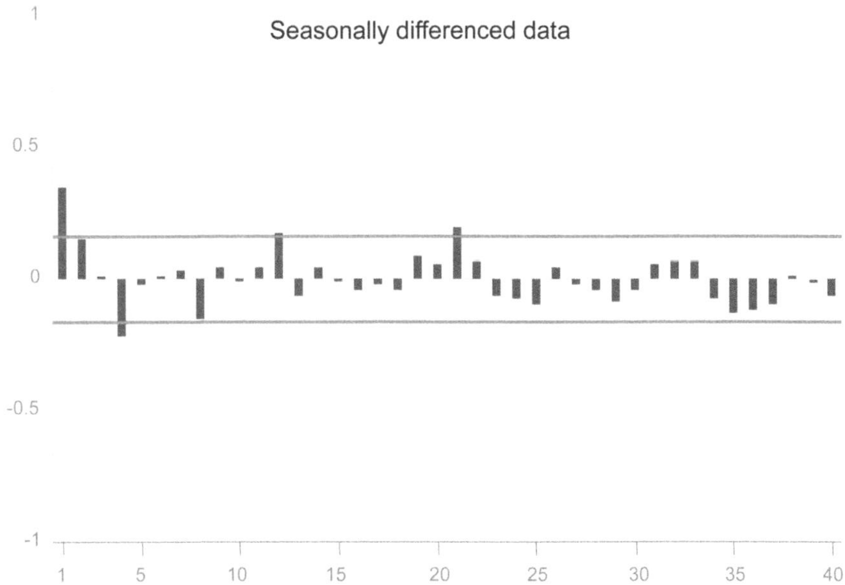

Figure 6.15 Auto correlation function

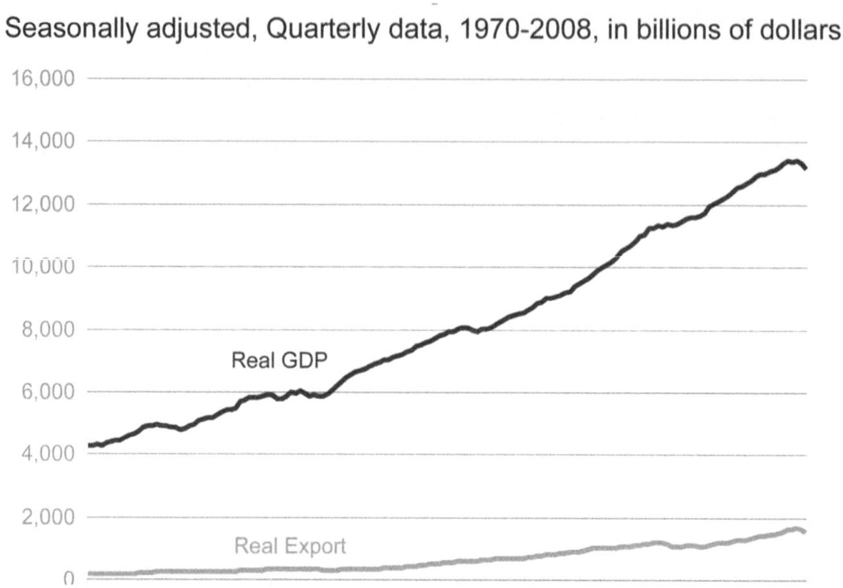

Figure 6.16 Partial auto correlation function

Table 6.6 Estimation results of the model: (0,0,1)*(0,1,0)

Parameter	Estimates	Std. Error	Std. Error of the Model
Constant	0.056375	0.005952	0.045122
b_1	0.323405	0.096155	

Table 6.7 Estimation results of the model: (0,0,1)*(0,1,1)

Parameter	Estimates	Std. Error	Std. Error of the Model
Constant	0.057498	0.003568	0.042454
b_1	0.374886	0.094621	
c_1	–0.404397	0.096496	

Table 6.8 Estimation results of the model: Seasonal (0,1,1)

Parameter	Estimates	Std. Error	Std. Error of the Model
Constant	0.057298	0.003291	0.046078
c_1	–0.298564	0.099002	

Table 6.9 Forecasts results

Forecast Period	2006:1	2006:2	2006:3	2006:4
Original Data	11,289	10,892	13,536	11,438
Forecast from (0,0,1)*(0,1,0)	11,354	11,166	13,937	11,137
Actual-Forecast	–0.60%	–2.46%	–2.88%	2.70%
Forecast from (0,0,1)*(0,1,1)	11,549	11,179	13,998	11,475
Actual-Forecast	–2.27%	–2.57%	–3.30%	–0.32%
Forecast from Seasonal (0,1,1)	11,786	11,249	14,000	11,416
Actual-Forecast	–4.24%	–3.18%	–3.32%	0.19%

As shown above, the graphical analysis in addition to the prediction results indicates that the first two models perform better than the pure seasonal model. In particular, this can be seen in the forecasts as presented in Table 6.9 above, where the deviations (in percent) between the actual and the forecasted values are compared.

Case Study 2: Accuracy of Forecasting Models – Utilizing Seasonally Adjusted Data vs. Non-Seasonally Adjusted Data?

The question of whether to use seasonally adjusted or non-seasonally adjusted data when predicting the future is an important issue with respect to practical implementation. For example, after examining 111 time series, Makridakis and Hibon (1979) reported that methods using pre-filtered, i.e. seasonally adjusted data performed somewhat better than methods which dealt with seasonality directly (including ARIMA models). However, as argued by Bell and Hillmer (1984), these results are inconclusive. Moosa and Ripple (2000: 170), for their part, used a single series in their analysis and concluded "... the results may turn out to be different if we use different series".

Such analyses can be very important for the decision maker in practice. In particular, one might conclude that for some time series, a better forecast can be obtained from seasonally adjusted data, while for other series, the use of unadjusted data will perform better. Thus, if we accept the maxim *let the data speak for itself*, and forecast with *both* methods, we *might* obtain a better outcome regarding the forecast.

In practice, such analyses requires a number of steps:

1. Modeling *unadjusted* data by B-J *seasonal* ARIMA models and generating a forecast.

2. Modeling *adjusted* data by B-J *non-seasonal* ARIMA models and generating a forecast.
3. Re-seasonalising the forecast from 2, by means of applying seasonal factors.

As an example of the above, monthly data (1970–2005) on Electricity Consumption in Israel, are examined. The models that were chosen are *seasonal* ARIMA (0,1,2)*(0,1,1) for the original data and ARIMA (0,1,2) for adjusted data from X-12-ARIMA and TRAMO/SEATS. The models were selected by the traditional approach of observing the correlograms and by minimizing the AIC and BIC criteria. The results reported in Tables 6.10 and 6.11 suggest that: (a) models that utilized seasonally adjusted data performed better than the *seasonal* ARIMA model; (b) the model that utilized seasonally adjusted data from TRAMO/SEATS performed *somewhat* better than the one that utilized seasonally adjusted data from X-12-ARIMA.

However, as was previously noted, the results presented here are for a case study and other examples might generate totally different outcomes regarding the use of the procedures described in the paragraph above.

Table 6.10 Forecast comparisons

Millions of KWH		Seasonal ARIMA (0,1,2)*(0,1,1)		ARIMA (0,1,2) Data Seasonally Adjusted by X-12-ARIMA		ARIMA (0,1,2) Data Seasonally Adjusted by TRAMO/SEATS	
Forecast Period	*Original data*	*Forecast*	*Forecast -Actual*	*Forecast*	*Forecast -Actual*	*Forecast*	*Forecast -Actual*
Jan-06	4128	3876	6.51%	4035	2.32%	4038	2.25%
Feb-06	3509	3479	0.86%	3654	–3.97%	3682	–4.69%
Mar-06	3649	3418	6.76%	3543	2.99%	3568	2.27%
Apr-06	3284	3232	1.62%	3264	0.61%	3299	–0.44%
May-06	3689	3611	2.14%	3646	1.17%	3676	0.33%
Jun-06	3919	3776	3.79%	3764	4.11%	3812	2.81%
Jul-06	4426	4506	–1.79%	4521	–2.11%	4570	–3.16%
Aug-06	4653	4486	3.72%	4522	2.88%	4572	1.77%
Sep-06	4457	3978	12.07%	4107	8.53%	4109	8.47%
Oct-06	3802	3445	10.37%	3737	1.76%	3685	3.18%
Nov-06	3586	3409	5.19%	3435	4.41%	3425	4.71%
Dec-06	4049	3837	5.52%	3814	6.17%	3875	4.49%

Table 6.11 Criteria for measuring the accuracy of the forecast

Criteria for Measuring the Accuracy of the Forecast	Seasonal ARIMA (0,1,2)*(0,1,1)	ARIMA (0,1,2) Data Seasonally Adjusted by X-12-ARIMA	ARIMA (0,1,2) Data Seasonally Adjusted by TRAMO/SEATS
Sum of squared of errors	0.04380	0.01948	0.01355
Mean squared error	0.00365	0.00162	0.00135
Root mean square	0.06041	0.04030	0.03680
Mean of absolute errors	0.05027	0.03419	0.02938
Remarks	(a) note that the errors are in % of deviations from the predicted values.		

Case Study 3: Export-led Growth (ELG), Growth-led Export (GLE), Bidirectional Causality (BDC) or None? – Case Studies of Israel and United States

In this case study we examine the issue of bidirectional causality between seasonally adjusted real GDP and real export time series data. Before starting the

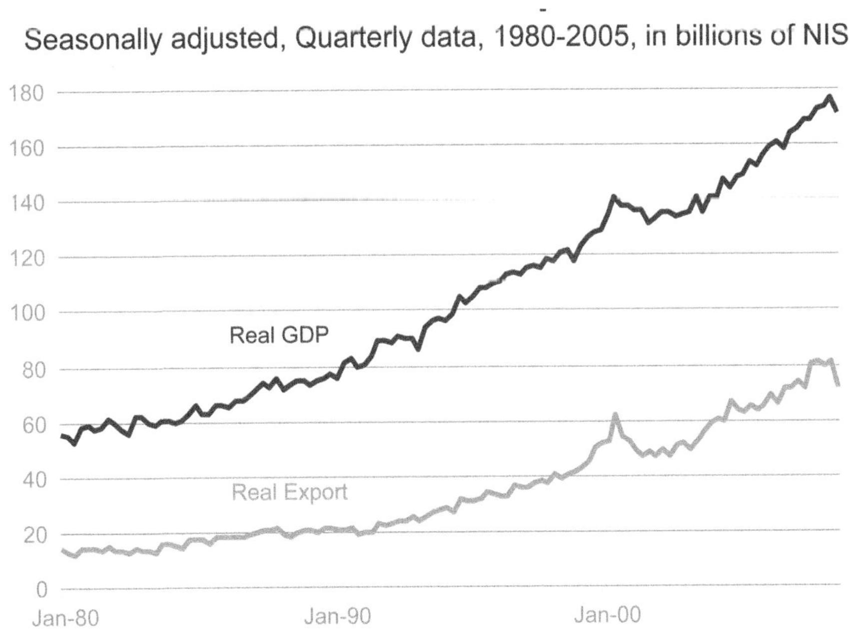

Figure 6.17 Real GDP vs. Real export in United States

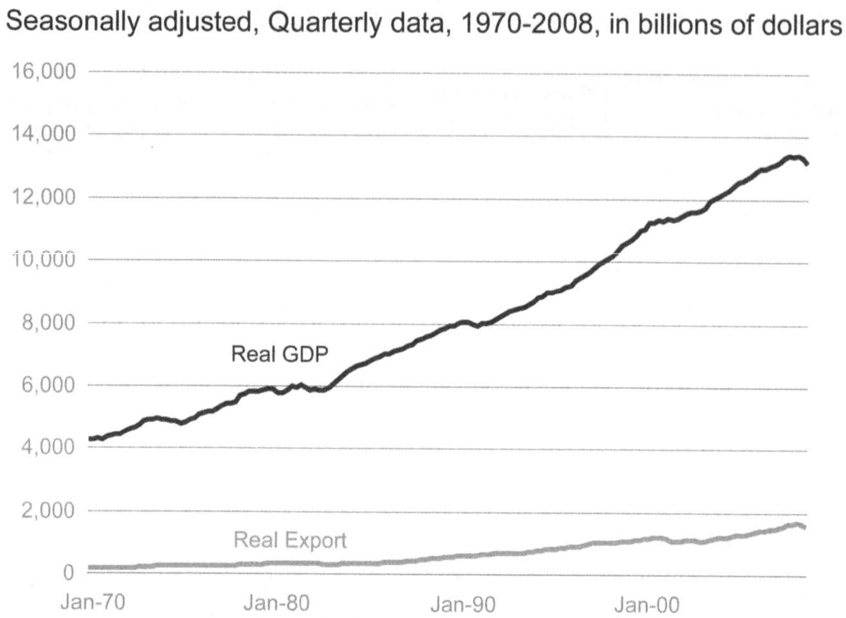

Figure 6.18 Real GDP vs. Real export in United States, seasonally adjusted

data analysis, the graphical evidence can give us a number of answers regarding the relationship between the variables. Both, US and Israeli data *do* drift from each other over time. This may indicate that the variables are *not* cointegrated. According to Engle and Granger (1987), if two variables are $I(1)$) and cointegrated (i.e. the residuals are $I(0)$), then we should expect the existence of *at least* unidirectional causality. In practice, according to Oxley and Greasley (1998), Konya (2004) and other writers, for a *bivariate system*:

(a) if variables y and x are $I(1)$ *and* cointegrated, then the following regressions should be estimated in the *level* form:[5]

$$(1)\quad y_t = a_0 + \sum_{i=1}^{k} a_i y_{t-i} + \sum_{i=1}^{k} b_i x_{t-i} + \varepsilon_t$$

$$(2)\quad x_t = c_0 + \sum_{i=1}^{k} c_i x_{t-i} + \sum_{i=1}^{k} d_i y_{t-i} + v_t$$

5 Alternatively, utilizing $I(0)$ data, we can include the Error Correction Mechanism which is discussed in Chapter 4, section 4.5.

(b) If y and x are $I(1)$ *and not* cointegrated, then the equations are given in the *differenced* form:

$$(3) \quad \nabla y_t = a_0 + \sum_{i=1}^{k} a_i \nabla y_{t-i} + \sum_{i=1}^{k} b_i \nabla x_{t-i} + \varepsilon_t$$

$$(4) \quad \nabla x_t = c_0 + \sum_{i=1}^{k} c_i \nabla x_{t-i} + \sum_{i=1}^{k} d_i \nabla y_{t-i} + v_t$$

Stationarity Analysis

The figure below, and over the pages that follow, first present the correlogram of the original data and then the correlogram of the differenced data. As it can be seen from the correlograms below, each time series, for both US and Israeli data is $I(1)$.

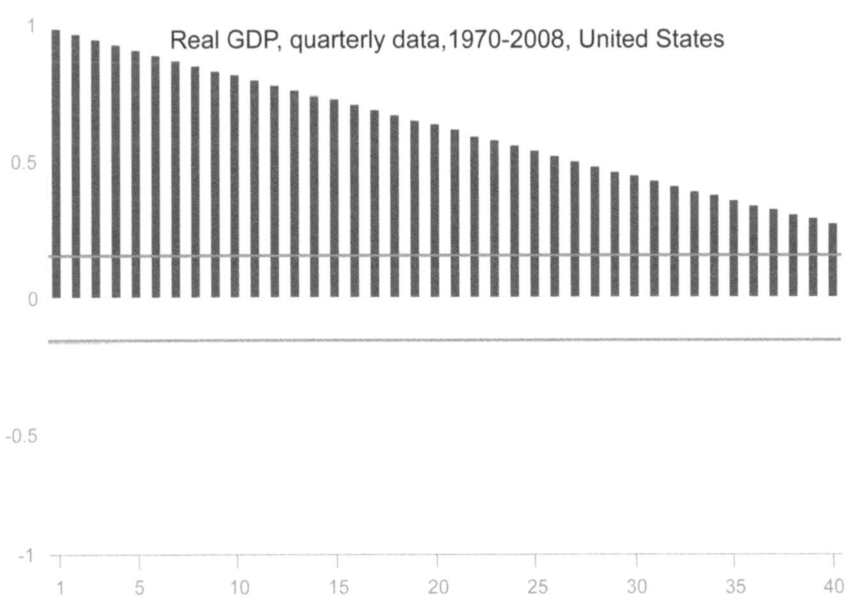

Figure 6.19 Auto correlation function, real GDP, US

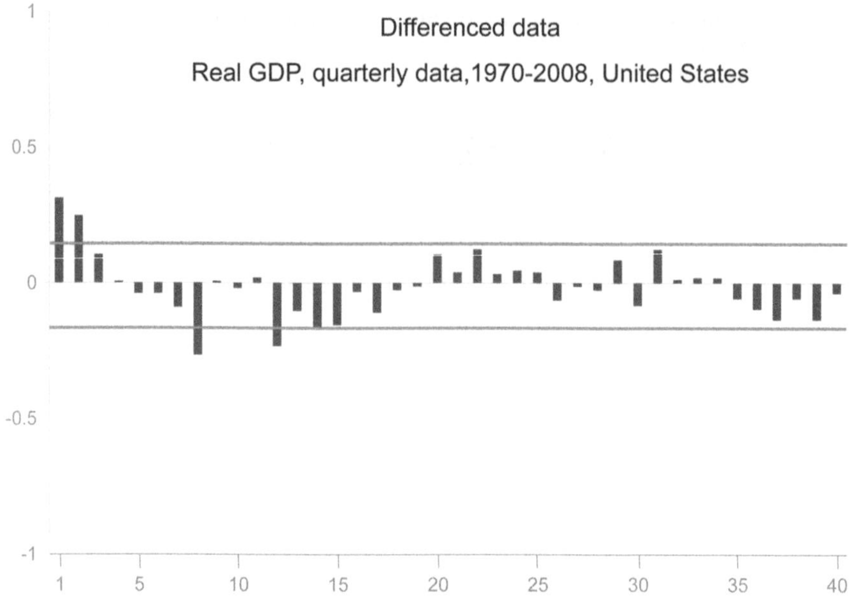

Figure 6.20 Auto correlation function, differenced data

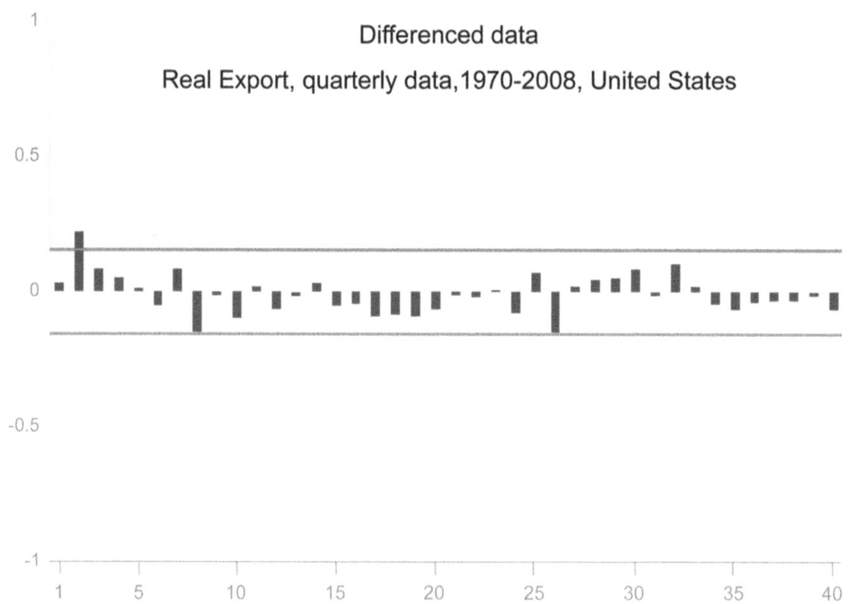

Figure 6.21 Auto correlation function, real export, US

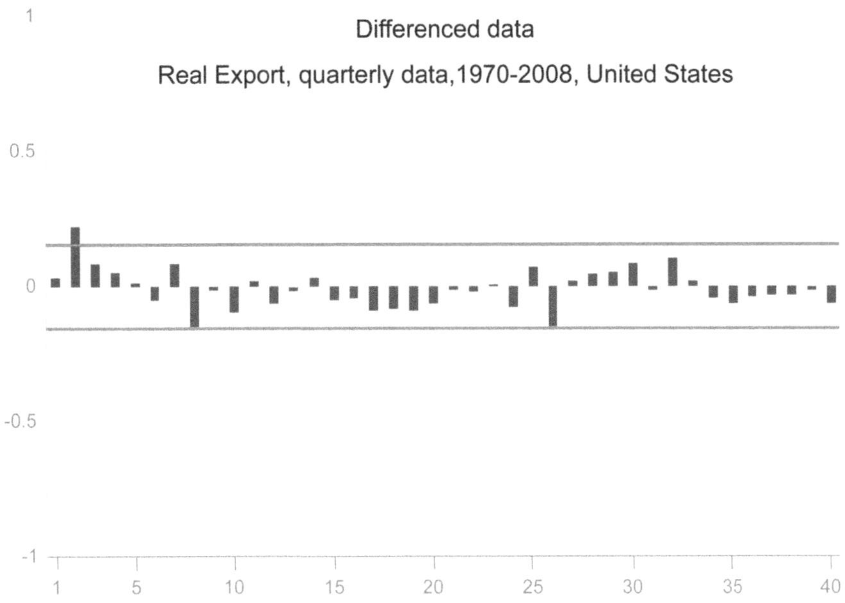

Figure 6.22 Auto correlation function, differenced data

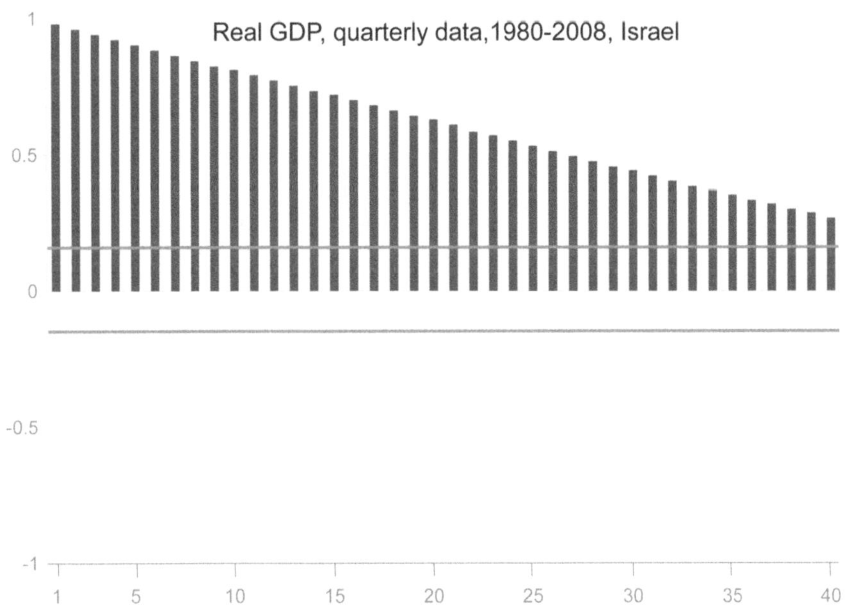

Figure 6.23 Auto correlation function, real GDP, Israel

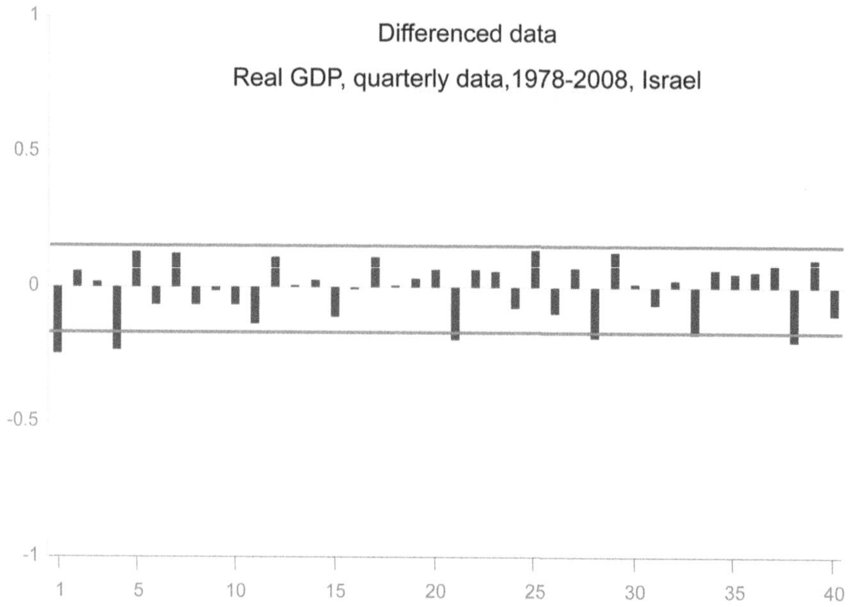

Figure 6.24 Auto correlation function, differenced data

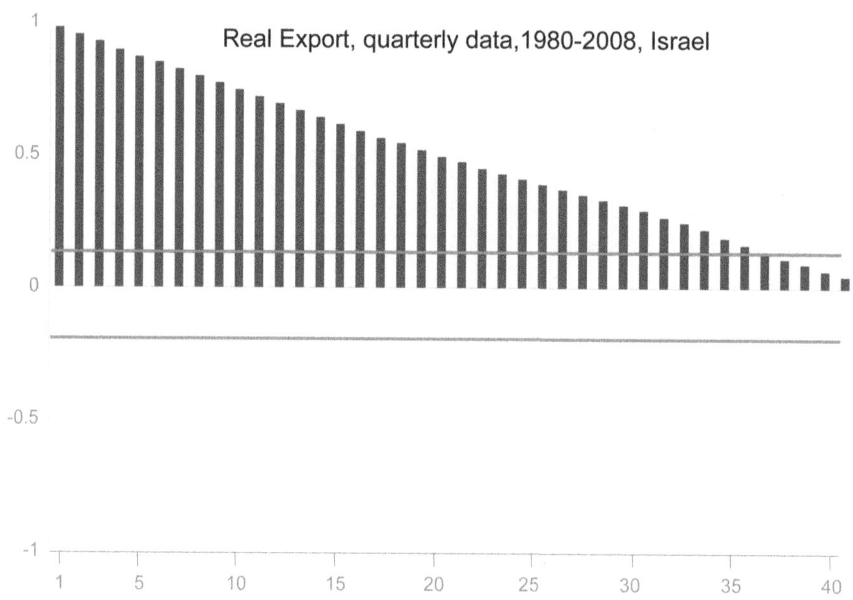

Figure 6.25 Auto correlation function, real export, Israel

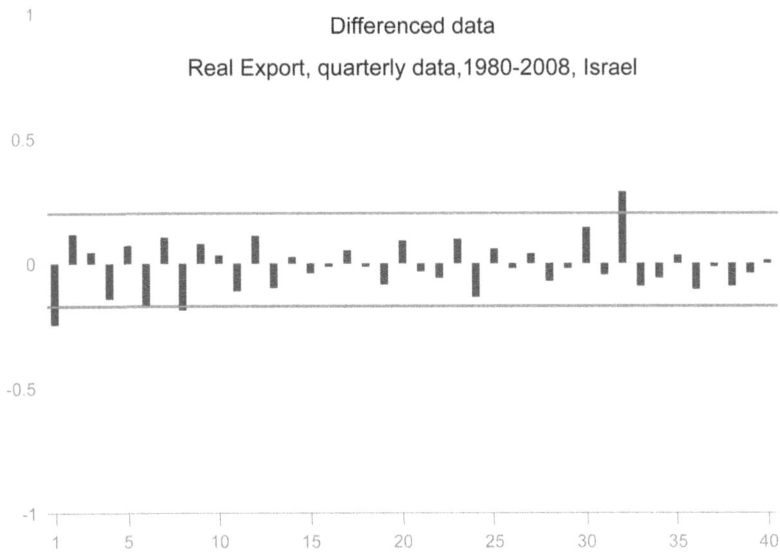

Figure 6.26 Auto correlation function, differenced data

The following step is to check the residuals of the model of the form that is given by $RGDP_t = \alpha + \beta REXP_t + \varepsilon_t$. As can be seen, the correlograms below clearly answer the question regarding the long term relationship between the variables, that is, the residuals are $I(1)$, and therefore, these variables are *not cointegrated.*

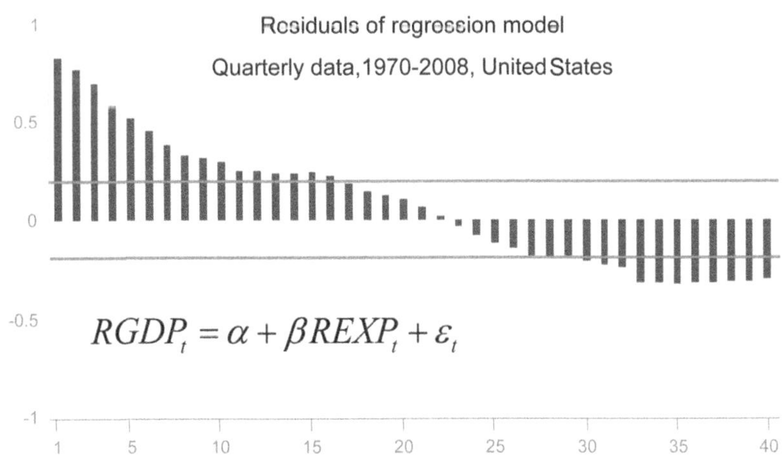

Figure 6.27 Auto correlation function, residuals of regression model, US

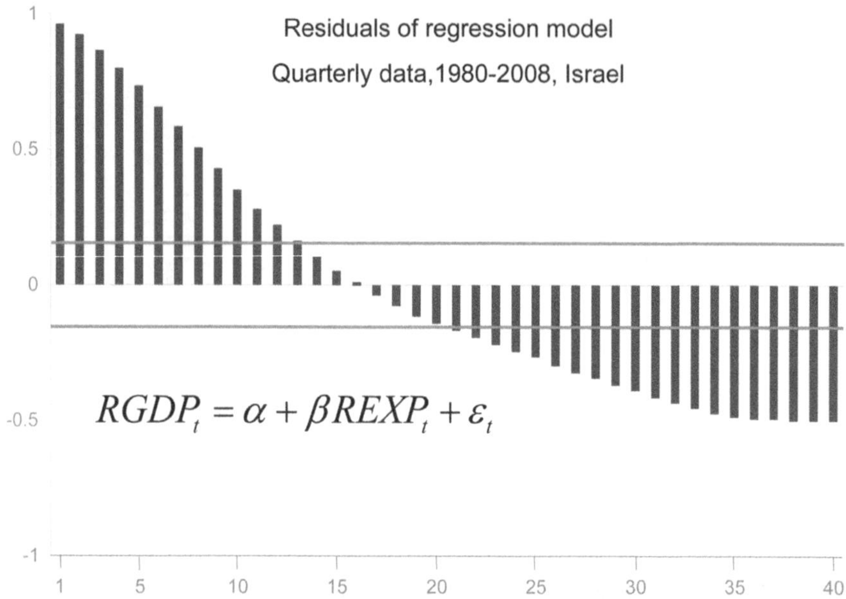

Figure 6.28 Auto correlation function, residuals of regression model, Israel

Since these variables are not cointegrated, to determine the direction of causality we utilize the regressions in *differenced* form (i.e. we have to check the relationship between the growth rates of RGDP and REXP, i.e., $\nabla RGDP_t$ $\nabla REXP_t$).

6.6 ESTIMATION RESULTS FOR DIFFERENCED FORM

The lag length selection is based on the values of AIC and BIC computed for each model. The procedure is followed by regressing $\nabla RGDP_t$ on lags of $\nabla RGDP_t$ *without* $\nabla REXP_t$, and the appropriate lag length is determined. Then, we include lags of $\nabla REXP_t$ in the regression *with* the *appropriate* lag of $\nabla RGDP_t$ and determine the appropriate lag length for $\nabla REXP_t$. The same is done in the opposite direction (Wahid, 2008). Nonetheless, there is a problem with this lag length selection procedure, since there is a possibility for sensitivity to the lag structure (Konya, 2004). Therefore, the more stable results are also reported, as can be seen in Table 6.12.

Table 6.12 Lag selection results

	US Data (*in natural logarithms*)				Israeli Data (*in natural logarithms*)			
Dependent Variable	Lag of RGDP	Lag of REXP	AIC	BIC	Lag of RGDP	Lag of REXP	AIC	BIC
RGDP	(1)	0	−1040.64	−1034.56	(1)	0	−570.88	−565.40
	2	0	−1034.69	−1025.59	2	0	−567.43	−559.25
	3	0	−1029.65	−1017.56	3	0	−561.45	−550.58
	4	0	−1029.57	−1014.49	4	0	−561.26	−548.71
	1	1*	**−1039.89**	**−1030.77**	1	1**	**−568.89**	**−560.68**
	1	2	−1032.60	−1020.47	1	2**	**−571.32**	**−560.41**
	1	3	−1028.42	−1013.30	1	3	−566.78	−553.19
	1	4	−1015.74	−1000.66	1	4	−561.28	−545.02
REXP	0	1	−679.57	−673.50	0	(1)	**−367.74**	**−362.27**
	0	(2)	−684.01	−674.92	0	2	−364.02	−355.84
	0	3	−677.48	−665.38	0	3	−359.66	−348.79
	0	4	−670.13	−655.05	0	4	−356.73	−343.18
	1	2	**−690.26**	**−678.14**	1*	1	**−366.12**	**−357.93**
	2	2	−690.16	−675.01	2	1	−361.92	−351.01
	3	2	−682.83	−664.68	3	1	−355.97	−342.38
	4	2	−679.64	−658.52	4	1	−354.64	−338.38
Comments	1) The values in parenthesis are optimum lags. 2) ** Contradicting results from AIC and BIC criteria. 3) * The *causality* coefficient of the equation is not significant at 90% or 95%.							

Causality – Country Results

The US and Israeli data provide interesting results, as can be seen from the following regressions (where: $y_t = \nabla RGDP_t$ and $x_t = \nabla REXP_t$):

US results: $x_t = \underset{(0.0036)}{0.0056} - \underset{(0.1334)^{**}}{0.0724}\, x_{t-1} + \underset{(0.0749)}{0.2729}\, x_{t-2} + \underset{(0.2048)}{0.7517}\, y_{t-1}$ (**– not significant)

Israeli results: $y_t = \underset{(0.0021)}{0.0110} - \underset{(0.1034)}{0.2117}\, y_{t-1} + \underset{(0.0458)^{**}}{0.0009}\, x_{t-1} + \underset{(0.3093)}{0.0924}\, x_{t-2}$ (**– not significant)

From a technical point of view we obtain unidirectional causality results, i.e. GLE relationship in US and ELG in Israel. However, the models may be affected by the lag structure and the fact that the data are in differenced terms.

Case Study 4: Relation between the Economic Growth and Electricity Consumption – The Case of Israel

The relationship between *energy consumption* and *economic growth* is well established in the literature. There are a number of reasons for the growing interest in this issue. The first is related to climatic change due to CO_2 emissions. The developing countries claim that they should be allowed to increase their emission of gases such as CO_2 more than industrialized countries, since they relate energy use to economic growth (Guttormsen, 2004). The second reason is related to developments in time series and econometric methodology. In particular, new tools can be utilized for analyzing the relationship between energy consumption and economic growth. Both of these tools that were discussed earlier, are related to *cointegration* methodology, and examine *causal relationship* among different variables. The latter is important since the *direction of causation* of this relationship (electricity consumption and economic growth) remains *controversial*, that is, results are mixed. There is a widespread literature that examines the relationship between energy consumption and real GDP, with different approaches and results. For further discussion, see for example Narayan and Prasad (2007), Narayan and Smyth (2008), Aqeel and Butt (2001), among other writers.

6.7 ESTIMATION

This analysis will be carried out in two steps. The first step is based on measuring the relationships between real GDP and electricity consumption with *seasonally adjusted quarterly data*. Next, this estimation will be carried out with *annual* data. In both analyses the data is transformed into natural logarithms. In addition two estimations of real GDP are considered. The first is based on *constant prices of 2005* (in NIS), while the second is based on the utilization of *consumer's price index* (CPI). For convenience, the real GDP will be denoted by "y_1" and "y_2" for time series based on constant prices and CPI respectively. The electricity consumption in Israel is denoted by "x".

Quarterly Data Results

Recall that both time series, x and y_1, were examined in case studies 1 and 3 above, respectively, and were classified as $I(1)$.[6] A short inspection of correlogram of y_2 below indicates that this time series is also classified as $I(1)$. Following previous procedures, these time series must be examined for cointegration relationship in order to determine the appropriate regressions for causality tests (regressions in the level or differenced form, as was discussed in Case Study 3).

6 In Case Study 3 the real GDP was based on constant prices of 2005.

Finding the cointegrating relationship is followed by the estimation of an OLS regression of the form $Y_t = \alpha + \beta X_t + Z_t$ which has the following results:

$$y_{1t} = \underset{(0.1310)}{9.5853} + \underset{(0.0058)}{0.6969}\, x_t$$

and

$$y_{2t} = \underset{(0.1679)}{8.2844} + \underset{(0.0074)}{0.7545}\, x_t$$

To answer the question whether the residuals, Z_t, from both regressions are $I(0)$ or $I(1)$, the correlograms are examined. However, as can been seen from the correlograms below, there is no clear-cut answer whether the series of the residuals should be differenced or not. Therefore, the ADF test for testing of the existence of unit roots in the residuals was utilized. The regression form that was chosen for the ADF procedure is based on the residuals and its partial autocorrelation figures, presented below. Specifically, partial autocorrelations of the regression residuals suggest that we utilize the first order autoregressive model for the ADF procedure, while the residuals' figures suggest a model without a constant. Thus, the regression form that was chosen for the ADF procedure is: $\nabla Y_t = \delta Y_{t-1} + v_t$. The results from the unit root analysis, presented below, give a clear answer regarding the residuals from both regressions. Thus, the residuals are $I(0)$ that is y_1/y_2 and x are *cointegrated*. Therefore, for the causality test, we have to use the regressions in the *level* form. As it was previously done in Case Study 3, the lag length selection for these regressions is based on the values of AIC and BIC computed for each model.

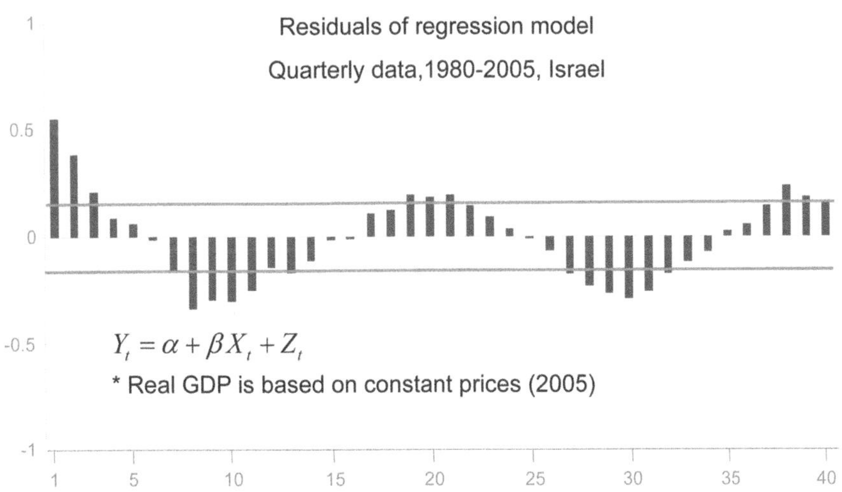

Figure 6.29 Auto correlation function, residuals of regression model, base='05

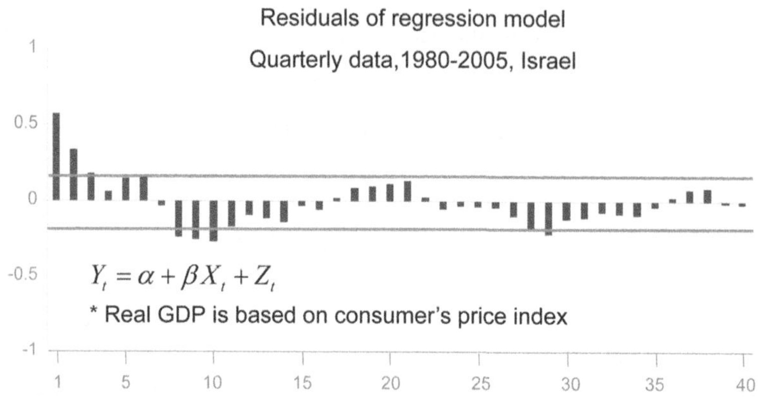

Figure 6.30 Residuals of regression model, residuals of regression model, CPI

Figure 6.31 Partial auto correlation function, residuals of regression model, base='05

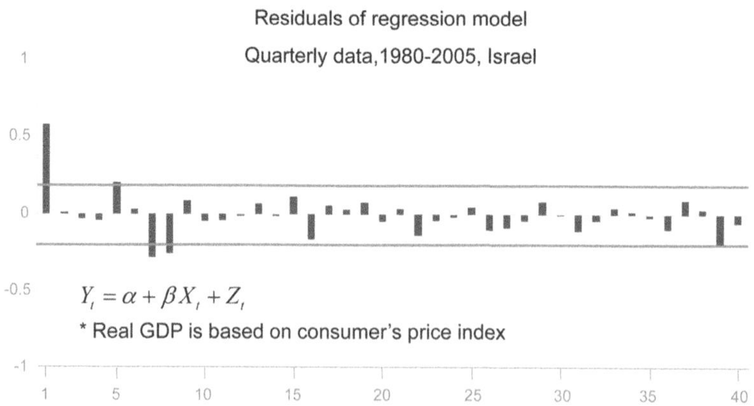

Figure 6.32 Partial auto correlation function, residuals of regression model, CPI

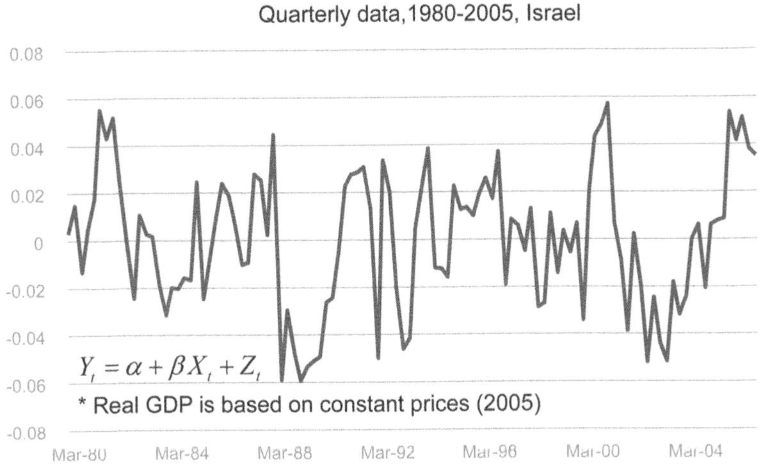

Figure 6.33 Residuals of regression model, quarterly data, base='05

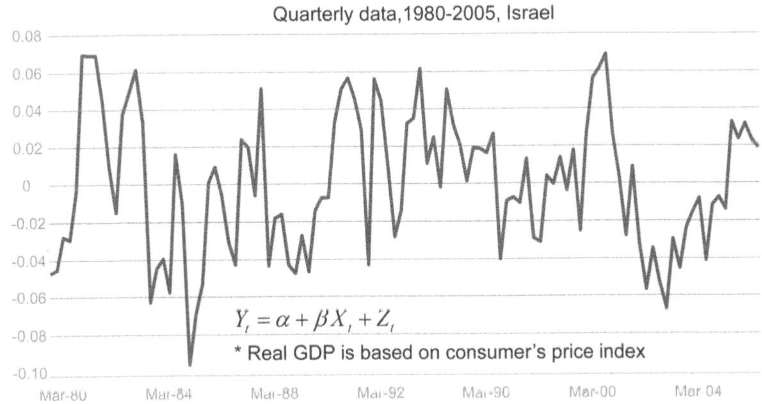

Figure 6.34 Residuals of regression model, quarterly data, CPI

Unit Root Results

The hypothesis and the decision rule:

$$H_0 : \delta = 0, (unit\ root)$$
$$H_1 : \delta \neq 0$$

If t* > τ (ADF critical value) $\Rightarrow$ unit root exists.

If t* < τ (ADF critical value) $\Rightarrow$ unit root does not exists.

Table 6.13 Unit root regressions

Regression Results	t*	τ	Conclusion
$\nabla y_{1,t} = \underset{(0.0813)}{-0.441} y_{1,t-1}$	–5.422	–1.941*	No unit root
$\nabla y_{2,t} = \underset{(0.0785)}{-0.423} y_{2,t-1}$	–5.382		No unit root
* Based on values given in Eviews program.			

Causality Results for Quarterly Data

$$y_{1,t} = \underset{(0.6690)^*}{1.3217} + \underset{(0.0689)}{0.8642}\, y_{1,t-1} + \underset{(0.0481)^*}{0.0941}\, x_{t-1}$$ (* not significant at 95%, but only at 90%)

$$x_t = \underset{(1.0916)}{-3.1933} + \underset{(0.1026)}{0.4904}\, x_{t-1} + \underset{(0.0926)}{0.2667}\, x_{t-2} + \underset{(0.1126)}{0.3442}\, y_{1,t-1}$$

$$y_{2,t} = \underset{(0.5815)}{1.3855} + \underset{(0.0685)}{0.8418}\, y_{2,t-1} + \underset{(0.0519)}{0.1164}\, x_{t-1}$$

$$x_t = \underset{(0.7229)}{-2.3755} + \underset{(0.0987)}{0.4885}\, x_{t-1} + \underset{(0.0894)}{0.2836}\, x_{t-2} + \underset{(0.0850)}{0.2976}\, y_{2,t-1}$$

6.8 ANNUAL DATA RESULTS

Following the procedures for the quarterly data the cointegrating relationship is followed by the estimation of an OLS regression of the form $Y_t = \alpha + \beta X_t + Z_t$ which has the following results:

$$y_{1t} = \underset{(0.2316)}{9.2217} + \underset{(0.0098)}{0.7412}\, x_t$$

and

$$y_{2t} = \underset{(0.4187)}{6.6702} + \underset{(0.0178)}{0.8485}\, x_t$$

The residuals of the regressions are classified as $I(0)$, as can be seen in the correlograms on the following pages. Thus, for the causality test, we have to use the regressions in the *level* form. Again, the lag length selection for these regressions is based on the values of AIC and BIC computed for each model.

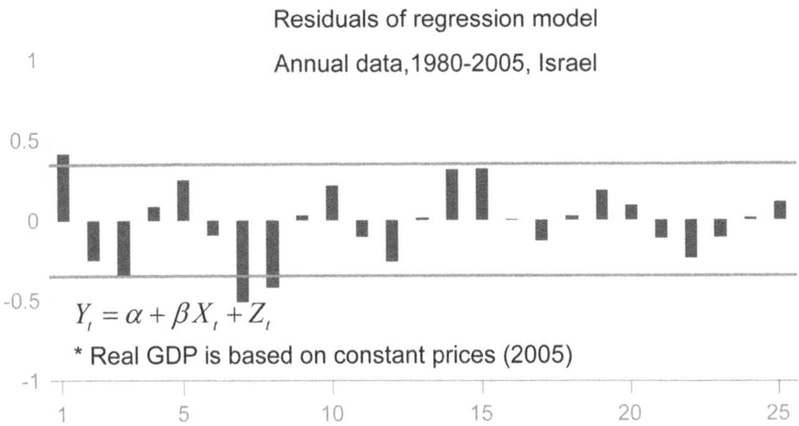

Figure 6.35 Auto correlation function, residuals of regression model, base='05

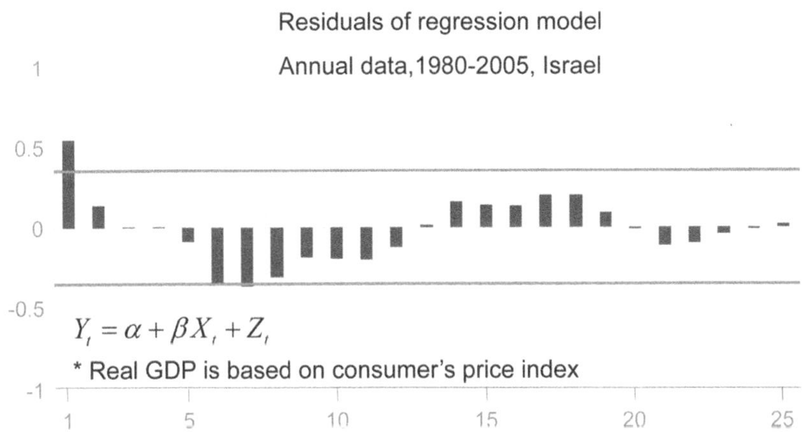

Figure 6.36 Auto correlation function, residuals of regression model, CPI

Causality Results for Annual Data

$$x_t = \underset{(2.2242)^*}{-3.4384} + \underset{(0.2368)^*}{0.3957}\, y_{1,t-1} + \underset{(0.1749)}{0.6999}\, x_{t-1}$$ (* not significant at 95%, but only at 89%)

$$y_{2,t} = \underset{(1.3821)^*}{2.6166} + \underset{(0.1959)}{0.6312}\, y_{2,t-1} + \underset{(0.1669)^*}{0.3081}\, x_{t-1}$$ (* not significant at 95%, but only at 90%)

Case Study 4 – Conclusions

One For quarterly data the regression results suggest a *bidirectional* and positive relationship between electricity consumption and real GDP, that is, they are jointly determined and affected concomitantly. This relationship is not surprising. On the one hand, Israeli economic growth resulted in expansion of the industrial and commercial sectors, where the use of electricity is essential. In addition, higher disposable income increased the demand for products consuming electricity. On the other hand, the growing demand for electricity reflects the *contribution of advanced production processes* – that utilize significant amounts of electricity – *to GDP growth* (Narayan and Smyth, 2008).

Two From the technical point of view, two computations of real GDP via constant prices and CPI, did with not significantly change the conclusions for the quarterly data. However, not the same can be said about the results for the annual data. In particular, once the estimation is made for the annual data, the loss of interior information in each year may be the reason for these significant changes in the conclusions. In addition as is shown above, the two estimations of real GDP *did* affect the direction of causality in the annual data.

6.9 SEASONAL ADJUSTMENT ISSUES

Case Study 5: Seasonally Adjusted vs. Non-Seasonally Adjusted Data and the Irregular Component – Case-Shiller Home Price Index in the US

The variant approaches presented previously should give the user the ability and tools to handle challenges in analyzing time series. Although seasonal adjustment makes it possible to better understand the fundamental trend-cycle of a series, the seasonally adjusted series *always contains the irregular component*, the magnitude of which can be crucial in drawing conclusions regarding the nature of the series, its fluctuations, and turning points. Therefore, in many analyses the answer lies within the original data rather than with the seasonally adjusted data. For example a structural modification like the introduction of a tax or an economic crisis, can be more directly observed in the original series, and must then take it into account, before establishing an adequate model of seasonal adjustment.

There are a number of home price index measures in the US. The US National Association of Realtors compiles an index based on median sales price of properties sold in a given period in hundreds of locations. However, these median prices may be skewed or distorted if there is a significant change in the composition of properties sold. For example, in periods when more or less expensive homes are sold, this would distort the direction of movement in prices. The US Federal Housing Finance Agency (FHFA) provides an index based upon sales financed by "Fannie Mae" and

"Freddie Mac" Federal Mortgage Bank mortgages and loans *only*. Thus, this index did not reflect the full extent of the US "housing bubble", *as it did not track sales of homes based upon subprime lending, or sales of houses above the limitations set by the Federal Mortgage institutions mentioned above*. The FHFA index, being *unit-weighted*, takes account of all sales *equally*. Standard and Poor's (S&P) Case-Shiller Home Price Indices tracks 20 major metropolitan areas, and these data are generated using a "repeat sales" methodology (see S&P/Case-Shiller Home Price Indices – *Index Methodology*, March 2008). The Case-Shiller Index, therefore, is that preferred by most business economists and housing-market analysts.

The next case study clearly shows the complexity of decision making using of SA vs. non-SA data. Two data sets are reported for the S&P Case-Shiller Home Price Indices – before and after seasonal adjustment. However, in order to track the decision-making process of S&P which was done at the beginning of 2010, seasonal adjustment was done on the basis of the 2000–2010 period, as can be seen in Figure 6.37.[7]

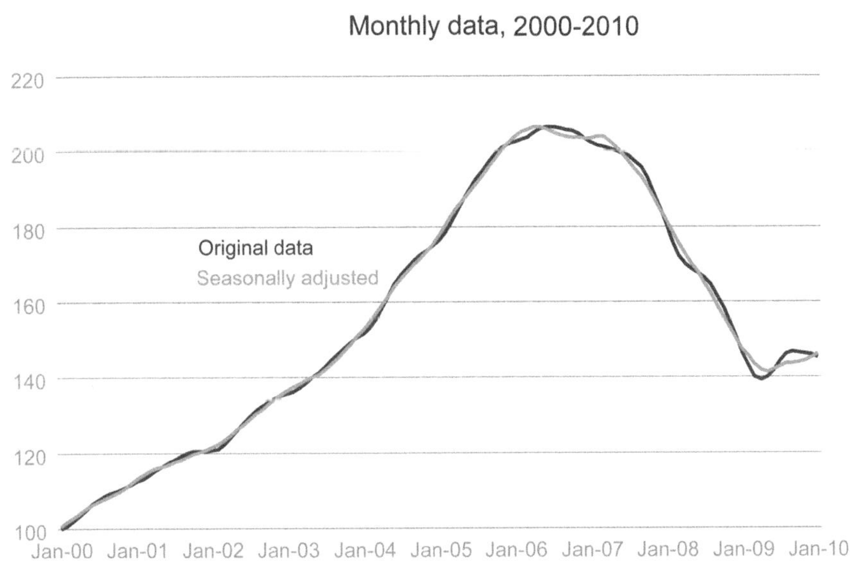

Figure 6.37 Case-Shiller Index, CPI

In April 2010, S&P reported that the two time series have given conflicting results. It can be seen for example in Figure 6.38 that if we take a *closer look* at the data

7 Seasonal adjustment computed by the authors here displayed no significant differences of seasonally adjusted data of S&P.

after 2008, generally at some points, the direction of SA data was in the opposite to the original. As a result:

> … the S&P/Case-Shiller Home Price Index Committee believes that, for present, the unadjusted series is more reliable indicator and, thus, reports should focus on the year-over-year changes where seasonal shifts are not a factor. Additionally, if monthly changes are considered, the unadjusted series should be used (2010: 1).

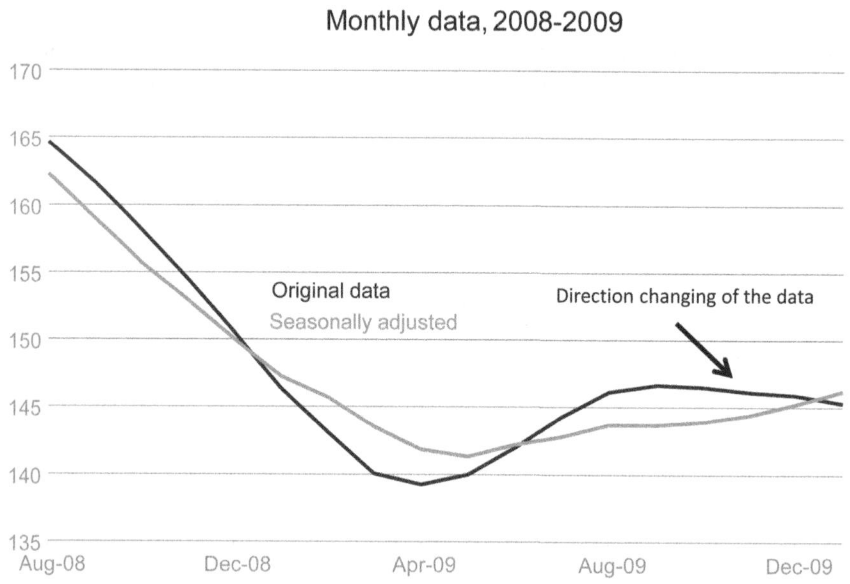

Figure 6.38 Case-Shiller Index, monthly data, 2008–2010

The S&P report also mentioned that they had no complaints about X-12 program which they used for seasonal adjustment, and stated:

> Rather, the turmoil in the housing market in the last few years generated unusual movements that are easily mistaken for shifts in the normal seasonal patterns, resulting in larger seasonal adjustments and misleading results (2010: 1).

Understanding this case is very important for the users of seasonal adjustment programs for practical reasons. If the *irregular component* of the data displays such volatile behavior, *it should be clear to the user that something unusual happened in the time series process.* This is seen in the irregular component of the series as in Figure 6.39 opposite:

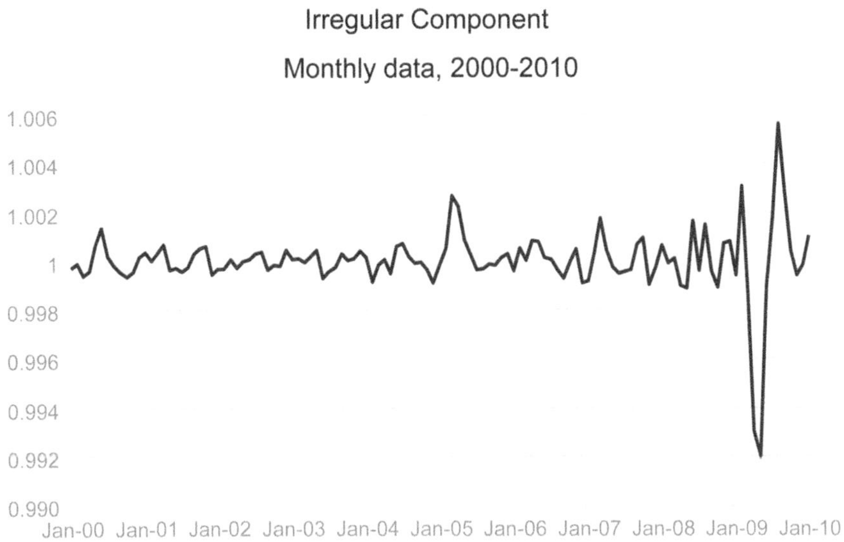

Figure 6.39 Case-Shiller Index, irregular component, 2000–2010

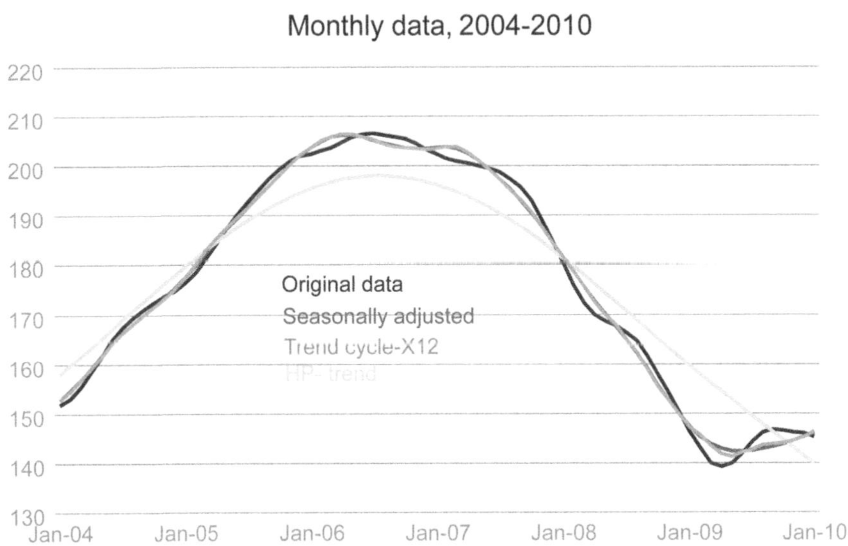

Figure 6.40 Case-Shiller Index, monthly data, 2004–2010

Just as an illustration of the impact of the volatility in the irregular component, as can be seen from Figure 6.40, the HP filtered data were able to describe the actual long run trend in the Case-Shiller Index of Home Prices over the period 2000–2010; this being due to the overwhelming influence of the irregular component in that period, as seen in the amplitude of its fluctuations as mentioned previously. The relative success of HP in this case is only due to the much longer period of smoothing that it reflects ex-post. On the other hand, the HP result was unable to correctly describe the trend between 2005 and 2010, where the CS trend cycle generated by X12 provided decent original data-tracking results up to 2009. However, in the short span of time from the middle of 2009, the direction of original and trend-cycle adjusted data moved in opposite directions.

In general, different series *may* display *some* "unusual behavior" at different points of time, that is to say, when the series might be out of "equilibrium" (i.e. natural long term behavior). This may result, for example, due to *outliers* or *trend breaks*. This is reflected in at least six months, or three quarters, of raised or lowered levels, as noted above. If the span of anomalous values is shorter than this, they are classified as extreme values (see Chapter 5, section 5.3). These periods, therefore, are crucial times for the user of seasonal adjustment programs who must be very cautious when using seasonally adjusted data, if at all. It is well known that many users "trust" the seasonally adjusted data provided by *official statistical agencies*. Whether this situation is *normal* is arguable, and will remain an open question. *Reliance on computer software may shorten the processes in decision making, yet there are cases when only common sense decisions can generate better solutions for data analyzers.*

6.10 EMPIRICAL EXAMPLES AND CASE STUDIES: CONCLUSIONS

As has been illustrated above, seasonal adjustment procedures are very useful tools for economic analysis. In particular, seasonally adjusted data reveal the *news* contained in the time series. *However, as was also shown, the results of seasonal adjustment often depend upon built-in options chosen within the adjustment program.* In particular, in a number of time series examples, the results showed that the TC component generated by the adjustment program can differ over short periods of time, *depending on the respective adjustment program.*

The accuracy of forecasting has been shown to be related to the choice of whether *seasonally or non-seasonally adjusted data are utilized.* In fact, the inconclusive results as reported above suggest that one can use – *albeit with judgment – either* seasonally adjusted or non-seasonally adjusted data, that is to say, pre-adjusted data in a non-seasonal forecasting model, or non-adjusted data in a seasonal forecasting model; once again, depending on the forecasting model and procedure chosen, *based upon the nature of the data and the maxim of letting the data "speak for itself".*

When dealing with dynamical relationship between variables, the superiority of one seasonal adjustment procedure over another is not the prime concern of analysis. As shown above, however, understanding the concept of stationarity, *is* crucial for analyzing macroeconomic variables and their interaction. The examples and case studies presented above illustrate the *synthesis* between the approaches of econometrics and time series analysis as manifest in the work of Box and Jenkins, Granger, Nelson and others, and *seasonal adjustment procedures* as seen in the contributions of Shiskin, Dagum, Maravall, Monsell among others.

CONCLUSIONS

This monograph focuses upon the history and the evolution of time series analysis. Over the years this area had made significant progress, from both theoretical and programmatic aspects. However, until the appearance of the now classic work by Box and Jenkins (1970), research on time series, on the one hand, and econometrics, on the other, seemed to be distinctly separate, in the sense that no synthesis appeared possible. The work of Box and Jenkins, and others, such as Granger and Newbold, changed the attitude of the economics community towards a purely statistical method of analysis and forecasting as suggested by Box and Jenkins and those who followed them. Indeed, over the years a substantial literature emerged, where the symbiosis between time series analysis and econometrics took place. A number of these watershed approaches are presented and discussed in this monograph, such as the work of Beveridge and Nelson, and Nelson and Plosser.

On a parallel track, the issue of decomposition of time series, and in particular the development of seasonal adjustment software algorithms, has provided a great service to users of empirical data. Nonetheless, this area is somewhat outside the interest and concern of the economics community. Simply put, users of economic data – such as economists – appear to be comfortable with pre-adjusted data, but it is doubtful that many of these users actually know and care about, or, for that matter, understand the methods by which the data is adjusted. Whether, this situation is a tenable one is arguable, and will remain open for further discussion.

In this monograph, an attempt is made to *understand* these pre-adjustment methods *and to demarcate* and *utilize* them in empirical analyses in a number of case studies. It was shown on a number of empirical cases that automatic procedures depends upon built-in options chosen within the program. Also, Case Study 2 examined the accuracy of forecasting models by utilizing seasonally adjusted data against non-seasonally adjusted data. This case illustrated why it is important for the economist to know the consequences of working with seasonally adjusted and non-seasonally adjusted data. In addition, much care has to be given to the choice of either working with filtered data or non-filtered data in a dynamic framework, since a wrong specification can severely bias the subsequent analysis.

To summarize the above, Lao Tzu (a sixth century BC Chinese poet) once said:

> Those who have knowledge don't predict. Those who predict don't have knowledge.

Indeed, sometimes, it seems that the situation is exactly as the poet said. However, these days it is not certain that knowledge for those who predict is not available. Rather, they may choose to *overlook* that knowledge....

REFERENCES

Akaike, H. (1973), "Information theory and an extension of the maximum likelihood principle," in B.N. Petrov and F. Csaki (eds) *2nd International Symposium on Information Theory*, Akademiai Kiado: Budapest.

Allard, R. (1974), "An economic analysis of the effects of regulating hire-purchase," Government Economic Service Occasional Papers, 9, HMSO: London.

Allard, R. (1975), "Hire purchase controls and consumer durables purchase," Department of Economics Discussion Paper 25–39–75, Queen Mary College, University of London.

Aqeel, A. and Butt, M.S. (2001), "The relation between energy consumption and economic growth in Pakistan," *Asian-Pacific Development Journal*, 8, 101–10.

Baxter, M. and King, R.G. (1995), "Measuring business cycles: Approximate band-pass filters for economic Time Series," NBER Working Paper No. 5022.

Bell, W.R. and Hillmer, S.C. (1984), "Issues involved with the seasonal adjustment of economic Time Series," *Statistical Research Division Report Series*, Bureau of the Census: Washington, DC.

Beveridge, S. and Nelson, C.R. (1972), "A new approach to measurement of trend and cycle components in economic Time Series," First Draft: Prepared for the Meetings of the Western Economic Association, Santa Clara, August.

Beveridge, S. and Nelson, C.R. (1977), "A new approach to measurement of trend and cycle components in economic Time Series," (draft manuscript, August 1977).

Beveridge, S. and Nelson, C.R. (1981), "A new approach to decomposition of economic Time Series into permanent and transitory components with particular attention to measurement of the 'business cycle'," *Journal of Monetary Economics*, 7, 151–74.

Box, G.E.P. and Cox, D.R. (1964), "An analysis of transformations," *Journal of the Royal Statistical Society B*, 26, 211–52.

Box, G.E.P., Hillmer, S.C. and Tiao G.C. (1978), "Analysis and modeling of seasonal time series," in *Seasonal Analysis of Economic Time Series*, edited by A. Zellner, US Department of Commerce, Bureau of the Census: Washington, DC, 309–34.

Box, G.E.P. and Jenkins, G.M. (1968), "Some recent advances in forecasting and control," *Applied Statistics*, 17, 91–109.

Box, G.E.P. and Jenkins, G.M. (1970), *Time Series Analysis: Forecasting and Control*, Holden-Day: San-Francisco, CA.

Box, G.E.P. and Pierce, D.A. (1970), "Distribution of residual autocorrelations in autoregressive moving average time series models," *Journal of the American Statistical Association*, 65, 1509–26.

Box, G.E.P., and Tiao G.C. (1965), "A change in the level of a non-stationary time series" *Biometrika*, 52, 181–92.

Box, G.E.P., and Tiao G.C. (1975), "Intervention analysis with applications to economic and environmental problems," *Journal of the American Statistical Association*, 70, 70–79.

Breusch, T.S. (1978), "Testing for autocorrelation in dynamic linear models," *Australian Economic Papers*, 17, 334–55.

Brockwell, P.J. and Davis, R.A. (1987), *Time Series: Theory and Methods*, Springer-Verlag: New York.

Brown, R.G. (1963), *Smoothing, Forecasting and Prediction of Discrete Time Series*, Prentice-Hall: Englewood Cliffs, NJ.

Burman, J.P. (1980), "Seasonal adjustment by signal extraction," *Journal of the Royal Statistical Society*, 143, 321–37.

Burman, J.P. and Otto, M.C. (1988), "Outliers in time series," *Statistical Research Division Report Series*, Bureau of the Census: Washington, DC.

Burns, A.F. and Mitchell, W.C. (1946), *Measuring Business Cycles*, NBER: New York.

Caporello, G. and Maravall, A. (2004), "Program TSW: Revised reference manual," Bank of Spain: Madrid.

Christiano, L.J. and Fitzgerald, T.J. (1999), "The band-pass filter," Federal Reserve Bank of Cleveland, Working Paper No. 9906.

Cleveland, W. Dunn, D.M. and Terpenning I.J. (1978), "SABL: A resistant seasonal adjustment procedure with graphical methods for interpretation and diagnosis," in *Seasonal Analysis of Economic Time Series*, edited by A. Zellner, US Department of Commerce, Bureau of the Census: Washington, DC, 201–41.

Cleveland, W.P. and Grupe, M.R. (1983), "Modeling time series when calendar effects are present," *Applied Time Series Analysis of Economic Data*, edited by A. Zellner, US Department of Commerce, Bureau of the Census: Washington, DC, 57–67.

Cochrane, D. and Orcutt, G.H. (1949), "Application of least squares regression to relationships containing autocorrelated error terms," *Journal of the American Statistical Association*, 44, 32–61.

Dagum, E.B. (1978), "Estimation of changing seasonal variations in economic time series," Survey Sampling and Measurement, *Statistics Canada*.

Dagum, E.B. (1980), "The X-11-ARIMA seasonal adjustment method," *Statistics Canada*.

Dagum, E.B. (1988), "The X-11-ARIMA/88 seasonal adjustment method – foundations and users' manual," *Statistics Canada.*

Dagum, E.B. (1999), "X-11-ARIMA Version 2000: An update of the X-11-ARIMA/88 seasonal adjustment method – Foundations and users' manual," *Statistics Canada.*

Davies, N., Triggs, C. and Newbold, P. (1977), "Significance levels of the Box-Pierce portmanteau statistic in finite samples," *Biometrika*, 64, 517–22.

Demertzis, M. and Hallet, A.H. (2003), "Central Bank transparency in theory and practice," Royal Economic Society Annual Conference, Warwick University, 2003.

Dickey, D.A. and Fuller, W.A. (1979), "Distribution of the estimators for autoregressive time series with a unit root," *Journal of the American Statistical Association*, 74, 427–31.

Dickey, D.A. and Fuller, W.A. (1981), "Likelihood ratio statistics for autoregressive time series with a unit root," *Econometrica*, 49, 1057–72.

Dolado, J.J., Sebastian, M. and Valles, J. (1993), "Cyclical patterns of the Spanish economy," *Investigaciones Economicas*, 17, 445–73.

Durbin, J., and Watson, G.S. (1950), "Testing for serial correlation in least squares regression, I," *Biometrika*, 37, 409–28.

Durbin, J., and Watson, G.S. (1951), "Testing for serial correlation in least squares regression, II," *Biometrika*, 38, 159–79.

Elliott, G., Rothenberg, T.J. and Stock, J.H. (1996), "Efficient tests for an autoregressive unit root," *Econometrica*, 64, 813–36.

Engle, R.F. and Granger C.W.J (1987), "Co-integration and error-correction: Representation, estimation and testing," *Econometrica*, 55, 251–76.

Epstein, P. (1999), "Wesley Mitchell's grand design and its critics: The theory and measurement of business cycles," *Journal of Economic Issues*, 33, 525–53.

Fischer, B. (1995), "Decomposition of time series: Comparing different methods in practice and theory," *Eurostat Seasonal Adjustment Project.*

Findley, D.F. (2005), "Some recent developments and directions in seasonal adjustment," *Journal of Official Statistics*, 21, 343–65.

Findley, D.F., Monsell, B.C, Bell, W.R., Otto, M.C. and Chen, S. (1998), "New capabilities and methods of the X-12-ARIMA seasonal adjustment program," Bureau of the Census: Washington, DC.

Findley, D.F., Monsell, B.C, Shulman, H.B. and Pugh, M.G. (1990), "Sliding spans diagnostics for seasonal and related adjustments," *Journal of the American Statistical Association*, 85, 345–55.

Gilchrist, W. (1976), *Statistical Forecasting*, John Wiley: New York.

Glass, G. (1972), "Estimating the effects of intervention into a non-stationary Time Series," *American Education Research Journal*, 9, 463–77.

Glass, G., Willson, V.L. and Gottman, J.M. (1975), *Design and Analysis of Time Series Experiments*, Colorado University Press: Boulder, CO.

Godfrey, L.G. (1978), "Testing for higher order serial correlation in regression equations when the regressors include lagged dependent variables," *Econometrica*, 46, 1303–10.

Goldberg, S. (1961), *Introduction to Difference Equations*, John Wiley: New York.

Gomez, V. and Maravall, A. (1996), "Programs TRAMO and SEATS: Instructions for the user," Working Paper 9628, Research Department, Bank of Spain: Madrid.

Gomez, V. and Maravall, A. (1997), "Programs TRAMO and SEATS: Instructions for the user," Beta Version, Research Department, Bank of Spain: Madrid.

Gomez, V. and Maravall, A. (1998), "Seasonal adjustment and signal extraction in economic time series," Working Paper No. 9809, Bank of Spain: Madrid.

Gottman, J.M. (1981), *Time-Series Analysis: A Comprehensive Introduction for Social Sciences*, Cambridge University Press: Cambridge.

Granger, C.W.J. (1969), "Investigating causal relations by econometric models and cross-spectral methods," *Econometrica*, 37, 424–38.

Granger, C.W.J., (1978), "Seasonality: Causality, interpretation, and implications," in *Seasonal Analysis of Economic Time Series*, Economic Research Report, ER-1, edited by A. Zellner, US Department of Commerce, Bureau of the Census: Washington, DC.

Granger, C.W.J. (1981), "Some properties of Time Series data and their use in econometric model specification," *Journal of Econometrics*, 16, 121–30.

Granger, C.W.J. and Newbold P. (1974), "Spurious regressions in econometrics," *Journal of Econometrics*, 26, 111–20.

Granger, C.W.J. and Newbold P. (1976), "Forecasting transformed series," *Journal of the Royal Statistical Society*, B 38, 189–203.

Granger, C.W.J. and Weiss, A.A. (1983), "Time series analysis of error correction models," in S. Karlin, T. Amemiya and L.A. Goodman (eds), "*Studies in Econometrics*," Time Series and Multiplicative Statistics, in Honor of T.W. Anderson, Academic Press: San Diego, CA, 255–78.

Greene, W.H. (2003), "*Econometric Analysis*," 5th Edition, Prentice-Hall: Upper Saddle River, NJ.

Grether, D.M. and Nerlove, M. (1970), "Some properties of optimal seasonal adjustment," *Econometrica*, 38, 5, 682–703.

Guay, A. and St-Amant, P. (1997), "Do the Hodrick-Prescott and Baxter-King filters provide a good approximation of business cycles?," Center for Research on Economic Fluctuations and Employment (CREFE), Working Paper No. 53.

Guay, A. and St-Amant, P. (2005), "Do the Hodrick-Prescott and Baxter-King filters provide a good approximation of business cycles?," Center for Research on Economic Fluctuations and Employment (CREFE), Working Paper No. 77.

Guttormsen, A.G. (2004), "Causality between energy consumption and economic growth," Department of Economics and Resource Management, Agricultural University of Norway, Discussion Paper.

Hillmer, S.C. and Tiao, G.C (1982), "An ARIMA model-based approach to seasonal adjustment," *Journal of the American Statistical Association*, 77, 63–70.

Hillmer, S.C., Bell, W.R. and Tiao, G.C. (1983), "Modeling considerations in the seasonal adjustment of economic Time Series," in *Applied Time Series Analysis of Economic Data*, edited by A. Zellner, US Department of Commerce, Bureau of the Census: Washington, DC, 74–100.

Hood, W.C. and Koopmans, T.C. (eds) (1953), "Studies in econometric method," A. Cowles Foundation Monograph 14, Yale University Press: New Haven, CT and London.

Hodrick, R.J. and Prescott, E.C. (1978), "Post-war US business cycles: An empirical investigation," presented at the 1978 meetings of the Econometric Society held at Chicago, August 30, 1978.

Hodrick, R.J. and Prescott, E.C. (1980), "Post-war US business cycles: An empirical investigation," Discussion Paper No. 451.

Hodrick, R.J. and Prescott, E.C. (1997), "Post-war US business cycles: An empirical investigation," *Journal of Money, Credit and Banking*, 29, 1–16.

Holt, C.C. (1957), *Forecasting Seasonals and Trends by Exponentially Weighted Moving Averages*, Carnegie Institute of Technology: Pittsburgh, PA.

Hurvich, C.M. and Tsai, C. (1989), "Regression and Time Series model selection in small samples," *Biometrika*, 76, 297–307.

Konya, L. (2004), "Unit-root, cointegration and Granger causality test results for export and growth in OECD countries," *International Journal of Applied Econometrics and Quantitative Studies*, 1–2, 67–94.

Kwiatkowski, D., Phillips, P.C.B., Schmidt, P., and Shin, Y. (1992), "Testing the null hypothesis of stationarity against the alternative of a unit root: How sure are we that economic Time Series have a unit root?," *Journal of Econometrics*, 54, 159–78.

Lee, H.S. and Siklos, P.L. (1993), "The influence of seasonal adjustment on the Canadian consumption function, 1947–1991," *Canadian Journal of Economics*, Canadian Economics Association, 26(3), 575–89.

Ladiray, D. and Quenneville, B. (2001), *Seasonal Adjustment with the X-11 Method*, Lecture Notes in Statistics, Springer-Verlag: New York.

Leybourne, S.J. and McCabe, B.P.M. (1994), "A consistent test for a unit root," *Journal of Business and Economic Statistics*, American Statistical Association, 12, 157–66.

Lipschutz, S. (1997), *Theory and Problems of Beginning Linear Algebra*, Schaum's Outline Series, McGraw-Hill: New York.

Ljung, G.M. and Box, G.E.P. (1978), "On a measure of lack of fit in Time Series models," *Biometrica*, 65, 297–303.

Lovell, M.C. (1963), "Seasonal adjustment of economic Time Series and multiple regression analysis," *Journal of the American Statistical Association*, 58, 304, 993–1010.

Lucas, R.E. (1976), "Econometric policy evaluation: A critique," in K. Brunner and A.H. Meltzer (eds), "The Phillips Curve and Labor Markets," *Carnegie-Rochester Conference Series on Public Policy*, 1, 19–46.

Macaulay, F.R. (1931), *The Smoothing of Time Series*, NBER: New York.

Maddala, G.C. (2001), *Introduction to Econometrics*, 3rd Edition, John Wiley and Sons, Ltd: New York.

Malinvaud, E. (1983), "Econometric methodology at the Cowles commission: Rise and maturity," abstracted from the *Cowles Fiftieth Anniversary Volume*, edited by Alvin K. Klevorick.

Makridakis, S. and Hibon, M. (1979), "Accuracy of forecasting: An empirical investigation," *Journal of the Royal Statistical Society*, 142, 97–125

Maravall, A. and Planas, C. (1998), "Signal extraction in non-invertible ARIMA models," Eurostat Working Paper No. 9/1998/A/6.

Meyer, M. and Winker, P. (2005), "Using HP filtered data for econometric analysis: Some evidence from Monte Carlo simulations," *Advances in Statistical Analysis*, 89, 3, 303–20.

Mills, T.C. (1990), *Time Series Techniques for Economists*, Cambridge University Press: Cambridge.

Monsell, B.C. (2006), "Advances in seasonal adjustment software at the US census bureau," Conference on Seasonality, Seasonal Adjustment and Their Implications for Short-Term Analysis and Forecasting, Luxembourg, 10–12 May, 2006.

Monsell, B.C., Aston, J.A.D. and Koopman, S.J. (2003), "*Toward X-13?*," Bureau of the Census: Washington, DC.

Montoya, L.A. and de Haan, J. (2007), "Regional business cycle synchronization in Europe," Bruges European Economic Research Papers No. 11.

Moosa, I.A. and Ripple, R.D. (2000), "The effect of seasonal adjustment on the accuracy of forecasting US West Coast oil imports," *Journal of Economics Research*, 5, 149–72.

Narayan, P.K. and Prasad, A. (2007), "Electricity-consumption real GDP nexus: Evidence from a bootstrapped causality test for 20 OECD countries," *Energy Policy*, 36, 910–18.

Narayan, P.K. and Smyth, R. (2008), "Multivariate Granger causality between electricity consumption, exports and GDP: Evidence from a panel of middle-eastern countries," *Energy Policy*, 37, 229–36.

Nazem, S.M. (1988), *Applied Time Series for Business and Economic Forecasting*, Marcel Dekker, Inc.: New York and Basel.

Nelson, C.R. (1973), *Applied Time Series Analysis: For Managerial Forecasting*, Holden-Day: San-Francisco, CA.

Nelson, C.R. (2006), "The Beveridge-Nelson decomposition in retrospect and prospect" (draft manuscript, July).

Nelson, C.R. (2008), "The Beveridge-Nelson decomposition in retrospect and prospect," *Journal of Econometrics*, 146, 202–6.

Nelson, C.R. and Kang, H. (1981), "Spurious periodicity in inappropriately detrended Time Series," *Econometrica*, 49, 741–51.

Nelson, C.R. and Plosser, C.I. (1982), "Trends and random walk in macroeconomic Time Series: Some evidence and implications," *Journal of Monetary Economics*, 10, 139–62.

Oh, K.H., Zivot, E.W. and Creal, D. (2008), "The relationship between the Beveridge-Nelson decomposition and other permanent-transitory decompositions that are popular in economics," *Journal of Econometrics*, 146, 207–19.

Oxley, L. and Greasley, D. (1998), "Vector autoregression, cointegration and causality: Testing for causes of the British industrial revolution," *Applied Economics*, 30, 1387–97.

Phillips, P.C.B. and Perron, P. (1988), "Testing for a unit root in Time Series regressions," *Biometrika*, 75, 335–46.

Pierce, D.A. (1975), "On trend and autocorrelation," *Communications in Statistics*, 4, 163–75.

Planas, C. (1998), "The analysis of seasonality in economic statistics: A survey of recent developments," *Eurostat: Luxembourg.*

Plosser, C.I. (1981), "Short-term forecasting and seasonal adjustment," *Journal of American Statistical Association*, 74, 15–24.

Prais, S.J. and Winsten, C.B. (1954), "Trend estimators and serial correlation," Cowles Commission Discussion Paper No. 373, Chicago, IL.

Prescott, E.C. (2004), "The transformation of macroeconomic policy and research," Nobel Prize Lecture, December 8, 2004. Arizona State University, Tempe and Federal Reserve Bank of Minneapolis, MN.

Prescott, E.C. (2006), "The transformation of macroeconomic policy and research," Nobel Prize Lecture, *Journal of Political Economy*, 114, 2, 203–35.

Quenouille, M.H. (1949), "Approximate test of correlation in Time Series," *Journal of the Royal Statistical Society*, Ser. B11, 68–84.

Rosenblatt, H.M. (1968), "Spectral evaluation of BLS and census revised seasonal adjustment procedures," *Journal of the American Statistical Association*, 63, 322, 472–501.

S&P/Case-Shiller (2008), "Home price indices," *Index Methodology*, March.

S&P/Case-Shiller (2010), "Index analysis," *Home Price Indices and Seasonal Adjustment*, April.

Said, E. and Dickey, D.A. (1984), "Testing for unit roots in autoregressive moving average models of unknown order," *Biometrika*, 71, 599–607.

Schwartz, G. (1978), "Estimating the dimension of a model," *Annals of Statistics*, 6, 2, 461–64.

Shiskin, J., Young, A.H. and Musgrave, J.C. (1967), "The X11 variant of the census method II seasonal adjustment program," Technical Paper 15, Bureau of the Census: Washington, DC.

Sims, C.A. (1974), "Seasonality in regression," *Journal of the American Statistical Association*, 69, 347, 618–26.

Slutzky, E. (1937), "The summation of random causes as the source of cyclic processes," *Econometrica*, 5, 2, 105–46.

Thomas, J.J. and Wallis, K.F. (1971), "Seasonal variation in regression analysis," *Journal of the Royal Statistical Society*, Series A (General), 134, 1, 57–72.

Wahid, A.N.M. (2008), "An empirical investigation of the nexus between tax revenue and government spending: The case of Turkey," *International Research Journal of Finance and Economics*, 16, 46–51.

Winters, P.R. (1960), "Forecasting sales by exponentially weighted moving averages," *Management Science*, 6, 3, 324–42.

Yamane, T. (1968), *Mathematics for Economists: An Elementary Survey*, 2nd Edition, Prentice-Hall, Inc.: Englewood Cliffs, NJ.

Young, A. (1965), *Estimating Trading Day Variation in Monthly Economic Time Series*, US Department of Commerce, Bureau of the Census: Washington, DC.

Young, W.L. (1977), "The Box-Jenkins approach to Time Series analysis and forecasting: Principles and applications," *Revue Francaise de Automatique*, Information et Recherche Operationnelle (RAIRO) 11, 2, 129–43.

Yule, G.U. (1927). "On a method of investigating periodicities in disturbed series, with special reference to Wolfer's Sunspot Numbers," *Philosophical Transactions of the Royal Society A: Mathematical, Physical and Engineering Sciences*, 226, (636–46), 267–97.

Zarnowitz, V. and Ozyildirim, A. (2002), "Time series decomposition and measurement of business cycles, trends and growth cycles," Working Paper No. 8736, National Bureau of Economic Research, Cambridge MA, January.

Time Series Econometrics, "Cointegration and autoregressive conditional heteroskedasticity," *The Royal Swedish Academy of Sciences* (2003).

"An introductory course on Time Series analysis – Electronic delivery," 2005, Information Paper, Australian Bureau of Statistics.

RELATED WEB SITES

Library of Economics and Liberty – www.econlib.org
Australian Bureau of Statistics – www.abs.gov.au
Statistics Canada – www.statcan.gc.ca
The Central Bureau of Statistics (Israel) – www.cbs.gov.il
Bank of Israel – www.boi.org.il
National Bureau of Economic Research – www.nber.org
US Census Bureau – www.census.gov
Banco de España (Bank of Spain) – www.bde.es/bde/en
Economagic: Economic Time Series Page – www.economagic.com
http://faculty.washington.edu/cnelson/macroeconomics.html

APPENDIX 1

BACKSHIFT OPERATOR (BO)

BO has a significant role dealing with algebraic manipulations when analyzing time series. We shall review some particularly important related concepts (see for example Box and Jenkins (1970), Nelson (1973), among other text books):

The BO is defined by:[1]

$By_t = y_{t-1} \Rightarrow By_{t-1} = y_{t-2}$

For instance, $B^2 y_t = B(By_t) = By_{t-1} = y_{t-2}$

More generally, $B^k y_t = y_{t-k}$, $k = 0,1,2,\ldots$ where $B^0 \equiv 1$.

The inverse form, $B^{-k} y_t = y_{t+k}$, $k = 0,1,2,\ldots$

Other useful operators are:

a) The difference operator: $\nabla^k = (1-B)^k y_t$, $k = 1,2,\ldots$

b) The summation operator: $Sy_t = (1 + B + B^2 + \ldots)y_t = \sum_{j=0}^{\infty} y_{t-j}$

We shall consider polynomials in the backshift operator

$$A(B) = a_0 + a_1 B + a_2 B^2 + \ldots = \sum_{j=0}^{\infty} a_j B^j$$

1 Sometimes the symbol L for lag is used instead.

where the a_j 's are constants. Operating on y_t yields a moving sum of y_t 's, which is given by:

$$A(B)y_t = (a_0 + a_1 B + a_2 B^2 + ...)y_t = \sum_{j=0}^{\infty} a_j y_{t-j}$$

LINEAR DIFFERENCE EQUATIONS WITH CONSTANT COEFFICIENTS

Difference equations, have an important role in time series analysis. For a further discussion see for example Goldberg (1961), Yamane (1968), and Brockwell and Davis (1987).

1. A difference equation is said to be *linear* if it is of the form:

$$f_0(k)y_{k+n} + f_1(k)y_{k+n-1} + ... + f_{n-1}(k)y_{k+1} + f_n(k)y_k = g_k$$

   where $f_0,...,f_n$ and g_k are functions of k, defined for $k = 0,1,2,....$ If the coefficients $f_0,...,f_n$ are constant then the difference equation is linear. If both f_0 and f_n are non-zero, then the linear equation is of order n.

2. A difference equation with the right-hand side that equals zero, i.e. $g_k = 0$, written as $f_0(k)y_{k+n} + f_1(k)y_{k+n-1} + ... + f_{n-1}(k)y_{k+1} + f_n(k)y_k = 0$ is said to be *homogeneous*.

3. In general, if the difference equation is of order n, and if $f_0 \uparrow 0$, then we can divide the equation by f_0 and obtain: $y_{k+n} + \varphi_1 y_{k+n-1} + ... + \varphi_{n-1} y_{k+1} + \varphi_n y_k = r_k$ where $\varphi_1 = f_1 / f_0, ... \varphi_n = f_n / f_0$ and $r_k = g_k / f_0$.

4. It is easy to find the solutions of the homogeneous difference equations (HDE) for which: $y_k = m^k$ $(m \uparrow 0)$. Substituting $y_k = m^k$ into HDE, we obtain: $(m^n + \varphi_1 m^{n-1} + ... + \varphi_{n-1} m + \varphi_n)m^k = 0$ where $m^n + \varphi_1 m^{n-1} + ... + \varphi_{n-1} m + \varphi_n$, is called the *auxiliary equation* (or *characteristic equation*) of the HDE. Thus, in order to find the solutions of $(m^n + \varphi_1 m^{n-1} + ... + \varphi_{n-1} m + \varphi_n)m^k = 0$, we simply have to find the roots of the auxiliary equation $m^n + \varphi_1 m^{n-1} + ... + \varphi_{n-1} m + \varphi_n = 0$ (based on Goldberg, 1961).

ALGEBRAIC POLYNOMIAL

Consider the quadratic equation which is given by $x^2 - a_1 x - a_2 = 0$. The roots of the equation, are easily calculated from the quadratic formula given by:

$$x_1, x_2 = \frac{-a_1 \pm \sqrt{a_1^{\ 2} + 4a_2}}{2}$$

The roots are real and unequal, real and equal or complex conjugate numbers if the discriminant is, accordingly, positive, zero or negative.

Before considering the case of complex roots of the auxiliary equation, we shall review some algebraic properties of complex numbers that may be unfamiliar (based on Gottman, 1981; Yamane, 1968).

COMPLEX ROOTS

When the number under the square root is negative, it does not represent any real number. Therefore, it is necessary to define an *imaginary number*, such that its square is negative and written as $i^2 = -1$.

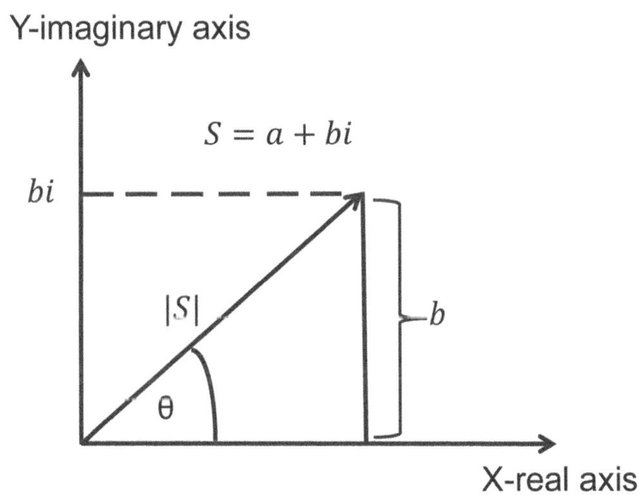

Figure A.1.1 Complex Plane

1. A complex number S is a sum of a real number, a, and an imaginary number bi, which is written as $S = a + bi$.

2. The length of the line from the origin to the end point represented by S is denoted as $|S|$, is called the *modulus* of the complex number S, which by the Pythagorean theorem is: $|S| = \sqrt{a^2 + b^2}$.

It can be equivalently written as $S^2 = a^2 + b^2 = (a+bi)(a-bi)$, where $S^* = a - bi$ is called the *complex conjugate*.

3. From trigonometric definitions, we know that:

$$\sin(\theta) = \frac{b}{|S|} \Rightarrow b = |S|\sin(\theta)$$

and

$$\cos(\theta) = \frac{a}{|S|} \Rightarrow a = |S|\cos(\theta)$$

Therefore, we can write any complex number as:

$$S = |S|\cos(\theta) + i|S|\sin(\theta) = |S|\left[\cos(\theta) + i\sin(\theta)\right]$$

4. By *Euler theorem*, it can be shown that $\cos(\theta) + i\sin(\theta) = e^{i\theta}$.[2] For negative values of θ the latter equation is $\cos(\theta) - i\sin(\theta) = e^{-i\theta}$. Combining, the previous two equations we obtain the following (based on Gottman, 1981; Yamane, 1968):

$$\cos(\theta) = \frac{e^{i\theta} + e^{-i\theta}}{2}, \quad \sin(\theta) = \frac{e^{i\theta} - e^{-i\theta}}{2i}$$

---

2 The exponential function and the trigonometric functions of a real or a complex number, z, are defined in terms of the following infinite series:

$$e^z = 1 + \frac{z}{1!} + \frac{z^2}{2!} + \ldots \frac{z^n}{n!}$$

$$\cos(z) = 1 - \frac{z^2}{2!} + \frac{z^4}{4!} - \ldots + (-1)^n \frac{z^{2n}}{(2n)!} + \ldots$$

$$\cos(z) = z - \frac{z^3}{3!} + \frac{z^5}{5!} - \ldots + (-1)^n \frac{z^{2n+1}}{(2n+1)!} + \ldots$$

APPENDIX 2

STOCHASTIC PROCESS

Instead of dealing with only one possible "reality" of how the process might evolve under time, in a stochastic process there is some *indeterminacy* in its future evolution, as described by probability distributions. This means that even if the initial condition is known, there cannot be a single rule for generating the precise value of the process at a given time. Let us present a more formal definition.

A stochastic process $y = \{y(t), t \in T\}$ is a collection of random variables. That is, for each t in the index set T, $y(t)$ is a random variable. The outcome of a stochastic process forms a sequence of real numbers, which we can also write as y_t. That sequence of real numbers is also called a *realization of the stochastic process or a time series*. Our goal in applied time series analysis is to draw inferences about stochastic process based upon the realizations we have observed.

Stationary Stochastic Process

A very special class of stochastic processes is based on an assumption that the process is in a particular state of equilibrium, in other words, a *stationary time series is one whose statistical properties such as mean, variance, etc. are all constant over time.* Most statistical forecasting methods are based on the assumption that the time series can turn into one that is approximately stationary *with the assistance of mathematical tools*. It is relatively easy to predict stationary time series. You simply predict that its statistical properties will be the same in the future as they have been in the past. Formally speaking, for a stochastic process to be stationary, the following conditions must be satisfied:

1. $E(y_t) = \mu$
2. $E\left[(y_t - \mu)^2\right] = \sigma_y^2 = \gamma_0$
3. $E\left[(y_t - \mu)(y_{t-k} - \mu)\right] = \gamma_k,\ k = 1, 2, \ldots$

Expressions (1) and (2) represent the *mean* and the *variance* of the data generating process, while (3) represents the *autocovariance* at lag k.

The above mentioned equations can be estimated from the time series data as follows:

4. $\hat{\mu} = \bar{y} = n^{-1}\sum_{t=1}^{n} y_t$

5. $\hat{\gamma}_0 = s^2 = n^{-1}\sum_{t=1}^{n} (y_t - \bar{y})^2$

6. $\hat{\gamma}_k = n^{-1}\sum_{t=k+1}^{n} (y_t - \bar{y})(y_{t-k} - \bar{y}),\ k = 1, 2, \ldots$

[Based on Mills, 1990; Box and Jenkins, 1970; Nelson, 1973].

Autocovariance (ACV) Function

Equation (3) is known as ACV function. The behavior of a time series is derived from the ACV between any two observations, that is, it depends only on the number of periods separating them. In that sense, ACV results, are enough to determine which pattern of behavior the time series might have. The ACV function has certain properties, in particular $|E(y_t y_{t-k})| \leq \sqrt{E(y_t - \mu)^2}\sqrt{E(y_{t-k} - \mu)^2}$, by the Cauchy-Schwarz inequality (see for example Yamane, 1968, among other text books).

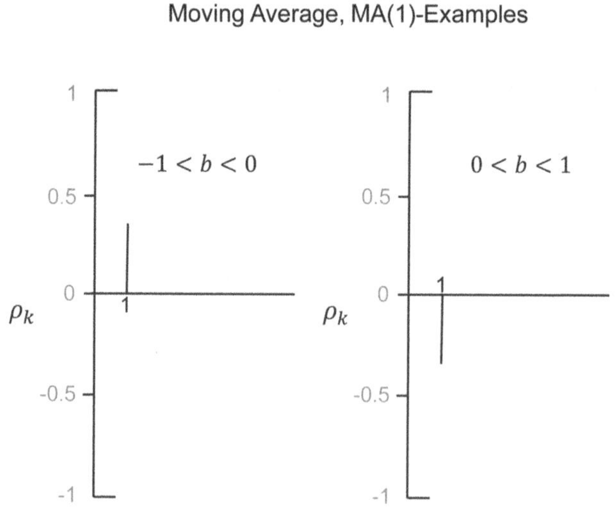

Figure A.2.1 Auto Correlation Function, Moving Average

Autocorrelation (ACR) Function

When our purpose is comparing different time series, then computing the ACV is not satisfactory, since the differences might be caused by different scales of measurement. As is well known, the variance is a measure of dispersion. Therefore, if our goal is analyzing the different series, it will require us to standardize the ACV function results by dividing them all by the variance of the process. This yields the ACR function, which is formalized as follows:

$$(7) \quad \rho_k = \frac{E[(y_t - \mu)(y_{t-k} - \mu)]}{\sqrt{E\left[(y_t - \mu)^2\right]}\sqrt{E\left[(y_{t-k} - \mu)^2\right]}}, \; k = 0,1,2,\ldots$$

From (7) we can conclude that:

a) The stationarity condition implies that the variance is constant over the time. Therefore, (7) can be presented as:

$$\rho_k = \frac{E[(y_t - \mu)(y_{t-k} - \mu)]}{\sigma_y^2}$$

or $\rho_k = \frac{\gamma_k}{\gamma_0}$, where $\rho_0 = 1$

b) It is easy to show that: $-1 \leq \rho_k \leq 1$.

[Based on Mills, 1990; Box and Jenkins, 1970; Nelson, 1973].

APPENDIX 3

GENERAL LINEAR STATIONARY PROCESSES

We shall shed some light on time domain models. The theoretical concepts will be discussed by examining the most practical examples of time series processes. For a further discussion see for example Box and Jenkins (1970), Nelson (1973), Mills, (1990), Nazem (1988) among other text books.

White Noise (WN)

WN is a sequence of identically and independently distributed random disturbances with a constant mean and a constant variance. However, for our purposes, unless stated otherwise, such a variable will have a mean of zero and constant variance of σ^2, or formally: $\varepsilon_t \sim WN(0,\sigma^2)$. Because variables in the WN sequence are not correlated, the ACVs at non-zero lags are all zero, or more formally:

$$(8) \quad E(\varepsilon_t \varepsilon_{t-k}) = \begin{Bmatrix} \sigma_\varepsilon^2, & k = 0 \\ 0, & k \neq 0 \end{Bmatrix}$$

Wold Decomposition

Definition – If a zero mean weakly stationary process y_t is *non-deterministic*, it can be expressed as:

$$y_t = \sum_{q=0}^{\infty} \psi_q \varepsilon_{t-q} + v_t$$

where:

a) ε_t is WN

b) $\sum_{q=0}^{\infty}|\psi_q| < \infty$ or equivalently $\sum_{q=0}^{\infty}\psi_q = K$, $\psi_0 = 1$

c) $E(\varepsilon_t, v_s) = 0 \ \forall s,t$

d) v_t - is deterministic

[Based on Brockwell and Davis, 1987].

First Order Moving Average Process – MA(1)

This process may be written as:

(9) $y_t = \varepsilon_t - b\varepsilon_{t-1}$, where ε_t is WN.

We can find immediately that:

(10) $E(y_t) = E(\varepsilon_t) - bE(\varepsilon_{t-1}) = 0$.

(11) $\gamma_0 = E(y_t^2) = E[\varepsilon_t - b\varepsilon_{t-1}]^2 = E(\varepsilon_t^2) - 2b\overbrace{E(\varepsilon_t\varepsilon_{t-1})}^{=0} + b^2E(\varepsilon_{t-1}^2) = \sigma_\varepsilon^{\ 2}(1+b^2)$

where the *cross product terms* (CPT) are given by:

$$E(\varepsilon_t\varepsilon_{t-i}) = \begin{Bmatrix} \sigma_\varepsilon^2, & i=0 \\ 0, & i \neq 0 \end{Bmatrix}$$

The ACV function is given by:

(12) $E[(y_t)(y_{t-1})] = E(\varepsilon_t - b\varepsilon_{t-1})(\varepsilon_{t-1} - b\varepsilon_{t-2}) =$

$= E(\varepsilon_t\varepsilon_{t-1} - b\varepsilon_{t-1}^2 - b\varepsilon_t\varepsilon_{t-2} + b^2\varepsilon_{t-1}\varepsilon_{t-2}) = -b\sigma_\varepsilon^{\ 2}$

The ACR function is given by:

(13) $\rho_1 = \dfrac{\gamma_1}{\gamma_0} = \dfrac{-b}{1+b^2}$, $\rho_k = 0$ for $k > 1$

The main idea behind (13) is that for example, observation, y_{70}, is correlated with its predecessor, y_{69}, and its successor, y_{71}, meaning that the "memory" of the process is one period long.

An alternative way to represent the MA(1) is by using the BO defined by, $B^k y_t = y_{t-k}$, $k = 0,1,2,\ldots$ where $B^0 \equiv 1$, as follows:

$$y_t = \varepsilon_t - b\varepsilon_{t-1} \Rightarrow \varepsilon_t = \frac{y_t}{(1-bB)} = \left[1 + (bB) + (bB)^2 + \ldots\right] y_t = y_t + by_{t-1} + b^2 y_{t-2} + \ldots$$

and if $b^j = a_j$ provided that $|b| < 1$, then the latter can be written as an *auto-regressive model of infinite order* as follows: (*) $y_t = a_1 y_{t-1} + a_2 y_{t-2} + \ldots + \varepsilon_t$.

From (13) we can derive that:

a) $-0.5 \leq \rho_1 \leq 0.5$, since $|b| < 1$;
b) it *cuts off* after lag 1, as it can be seen in Figure A.2.1.

At this point we shall define the next term, which will clarify the relationship between MA(q) and AR(∞).

[Based on Mills, 1990; Box and Jenkins, 1970; Nelson, 1973; Nazem, 1988].

Invertibility

Definition – A MA(q) process defined by the equation $y_t = b_q(B)\varepsilon_t$, is said to be *invertible* if there is a sequence of constants $\{a_j\}$ such that:

$$\sum_{j=0}^{\infty} |a_j| < \infty \text{ and } \varepsilon_t = \sum_{j=0}^{\infty} a_j y_{t-j}, \text{ provided that } |b_i| < 1 \text{ for } i = 1, 2 \ldots q$$

For example, we say that the MA(1) is invertible, that is, we can "invert" the MA(1) process and express its *current value* in terms of a *current shock* and *lagged observable values* of the series, provided the condition $|b| < 1$.

[Based on Mills, 1990; Box and Jenkins, 1970; Nelson, 1973; Nazem, 1988].

Second Order Moving Average Process – MA(2)

This process is given by:

(14) $y_t = \varepsilon_t - b_1\varepsilon_{t-1} - b_2\varepsilon_{t-2}$, where ε_t is WN.

Then, $E(y_t) = 0$.

The variance of the process is given by:

$$(15) \quad \gamma_0 = E(y_t^2) = E(\varepsilon_t - b_1\varepsilon_{t-1} - b_2\varepsilon_{t-2})^2 = E(\varepsilon_t^2) + b_1^2 E(\varepsilon_{t-1}^2) + b_2^2 E(\varepsilon_{t-2}^2) +$$

$$+ E(\overbrace{CPT}^{=0}) = \sigma_\varepsilon^2(1 + b_1^2 + b_2^2)$$

The ACV function is given by:

$$(16)\quad \gamma_1 = E\left[(y_t)(y_{t-1})\right] = E(\varepsilon_t - b_1\varepsilon_{t-1} - b_2\varepsilon_{t-2})(\varepsilon_{t-1} - b_1\varepsilon_{t-2} - b_2\varepsilon_{t-3}) =$$

$$= E(-b_1\varepsilon_{t-1}^2 + b_1b_2\varepsilon_{t-2}^2 + CPT) = \sigma_\varepsilon^{\ 2}(-b_1 + b_1b_2)$$

$$(17)\quad \gamma_2 = E\left[(y_t)(y_{t-2})\right] = E(\varepsilon_t - b_1\varepsilon_{t-1} - b_2\varepsilon_{t-2})(\varepsilon_{t-2} - b_1\varepsilon_{t-3} - b_2\varepsilon_{t-4}) =$$

$$= E(-b_2\varepsilon_{t-2}^2 + CPT) = -b_2\sigma_\varepsilon^{\ 2}$$

The ACR function is given by:

$$(18)\quad \rho_1 = \frac{\gamma_1}{\gamma_0} = \frac{-b_1 + b_1b_2}{(1 + b_1^{\ 2} + b_2^{\ 2})} \text{ and } \rho_2 = \frac{\gamma_2}{\gamma_0} = \frac{-b_2}{(1 + b_1^{\ 2} + b_2^{\ 2})},\ \rho_k = 0 \text{ for } k > 2.$$

This time, (18) implies that observations more than two periods apart, are uncorrelated.

[Based on Mills, 1990; Box and Jenkins, 1970; Nelson, 1973; Nazem, 1988].

General Moving Average Process – MA(q)

The general representation is given by:

$$(19)\quad y_t = \varepsilon_t - b_1\varepsilon_{t-1} - b_2\varepsilon_{t-2} - \ldots b_q\varepsilon_{t-q}, \text{ where } \varepsilon_t \text{ is WN.}$$

Then, $E(y_t) = 0$.

$$(20)\quad \gamma_k = E\left[(y_t)(y_{t-k})\right] = E(\varepsilon_t - b_1\varepsilon_{t-1}\ldots - b_q\varepsilon_{t-q})(\varepsilon_{t-k} - b_1\varepsilon_{t-k-1}\ldots - b_q\varepsilon_{t-k-q}) \Rightarrow$$

$$\Rightarrow \gamma_k = \begin{cases} \sigma_\varepsilon^{\ 2}(-b_k + b_1b_{k+1} + \ldots + b_{q-k}b_q) & k = 1,2\ldots q \\ 0, & k > q \end{cases}$$

$$\Rightarrow \gamma_0 = \sigma_\varepsilon^{\ 2}(1 + b_1^{\ 2} + b_2^{\ 2} + \ldots b_q^{\ 2}).$$

$$(21)\quad \rho_k = \left\{\begin{matrix} \dfrac{-b_k + b_1b_{k+1} + \ldots + b_{q-k}b_q}{1 + b_1^{\ 2} + \ldots b_q^{\ 2}} & k = 1,2\ldots q \\ 0, & k > q \end{matrix}\right\}$$

The MA(q) process requires estimating q+1 parameters, i.e. $b_1 \ldots b_q$ and $\sigma_\varepsilon^{\ 2}$.

This time, (21) implies that the ACR function cuts off after lag q. Observations more than q periods apart, are uncorrelated.

[Based on Mills, 1990; Box and Jenkins, 1970; Nelson, 1973; Nazem, 1988].

Autoregressive (AR) Process

We have shown that time series process can be approximated by a finite MA(q) model. Nevertheless, this representation is not unique and it is not always the most efficient one. Therefore, we will discuss AR process, and, in particular, its concepts necessary to understand the *duality* between MA and AR models. The conditions that guarantee transformation from an AR representation to a MA representation, are called *stationarity conditions* and from a MA representation to an AR representation, are called *invertibility conditions*. Consider the MA(q) process which is given by:

$y_t = \varepsilon_t - b_1\varepsilon_{t-1} - b_2\varepsilon_{t-2} - ...b_q\varepsilon_{t-q}$, where ε_t is WN.

Then,

$$\varepsilon_t = y_t - b_1\varepsilon_{t-1} - ... - b_q\varepsilon_{t-q}$$

$$\varepsilon_{t-1} = y_{t-1} - b_1\varepsilon_{t-2} - ... - b_q\varepsilon_{t-q-1}$$

$$\varepsilon_{t-2} = y_{t-2} - b_1\varepsilon_{t-3} - ... - b_q\varepsilon_{t-q-2},$$

$$\vdots \qquad \qquad \vdots$$

Repeatedly iterating, we obtain:

(22) $y_t = a_1 y_{t-1} + a_2 y_{t-2} + ... + \varepsilon_t$, which is the general AR(p) process.

[Based on Mills, 1990; Box and Jenkins, 1970; Nelson, 1973; Nazem, 1988].

Relationship between AR(p) and MA(q)

By utilizing the BO, (22) can be represented as:

(23) $a_p(B)y_t = \varepsilon_t$, where $a_p(B) = 1 - a_1 B - a_2 B^2 - ... - a_p B^p$

Recall that the MA(q) process can be written in the same manner, that is:

(24) $b_q(B)\varepsilon_t = y_t$ where $b_q(B) = 1 - b_1 B - b_2 B^2 - ... - b_q B^q$

Combining both (23) and (24) gives us:

(25) $a_p(B)b_q(B) = 1$

The relation expressed in (25) has important implications, since it may be used to derive $a's$ weights knowing $b's$, and vice versa.

[Based on Mills, 1990; Box and Jenkins, 1970; Nelson, 1973; Nazem, 1988].

First Order Autoregressive Process – AR(1)

This process is given by:[1]

(26) $y_t = \alpha y_{t-1} + \varepsilon_t$, $t = 1, 2, \ldots T$, where ε_t is WN.

By utilizing BO, it can be easily shown that (26) is equivalent to:

$$y_t = \sum_{i=0}^{\infty} a^i \varepsilon_{t-i}$$

provided that $|a| < 1$, which is the stationarity condition. Thus, the AR(1) model can be written as a MA(∞) model.

Therefore, $E(y_t) = 0$.

The ACV function is given by:

(27) $$\gamma_k = E(y_t y_{t-k}) = E(\varepsilon_t + a\varepsilon_{t-1} + \ldots a^k \varepsilon_{t-k} + a^{k+1}\varepsilon_{t-k-1} \ldots)(\varepsilon_{t-k} + a\varepsilon_{t-k-1} + a^2\varepsilon_{t-k-2} + \ldots) =$$

$$= E\left[(a^k \varepsilon_{t-k}^2) + (a^{k+2}\varepsilon_{t-k-1}^2) + (a^{k+4}\varepsilon_{t-k-2}^2) + \ldots\right] + E(CPT)$$

$$= a^k \sigma_\varepsilon^{\ 2}(1 + a^2 + a^4 \ldots) = a^k \sigma_\varepsilon^{\ 2} \sum_{i=0}^{\infty} a^{2i} = \frac{a^k \sigma_\varepsilon^{\ 2}}{1 - a^2}$$

For $k = 0$ we obtain $\gamma_0 = \dfrac{\sigma_\varepsilon^{\ 2}}{1 - a^2}$.

The ACR function is given by:

(28) $$\rho_k = \frac{\gamma_k}{\gamma_0} = a^k$$

---

1 This process is also known as the Markov process. Higher order AR processes are not Markov processes since they depend on two or more periods of time.

We have shown that under the condition that $|a| < 1$ the moments, i.e., the mean, variance and ACV are not time dependent, which means, that the requirement of stationarity has been realized.

From (28) we can derive the behavior of the ACRs as can be seen in Figure A.3.1. For $0 < a < 1$ we see an exponential decay toward zero, whereas for $-1 < a < 0$ it decays exponentially to zero and oscillates in sign.

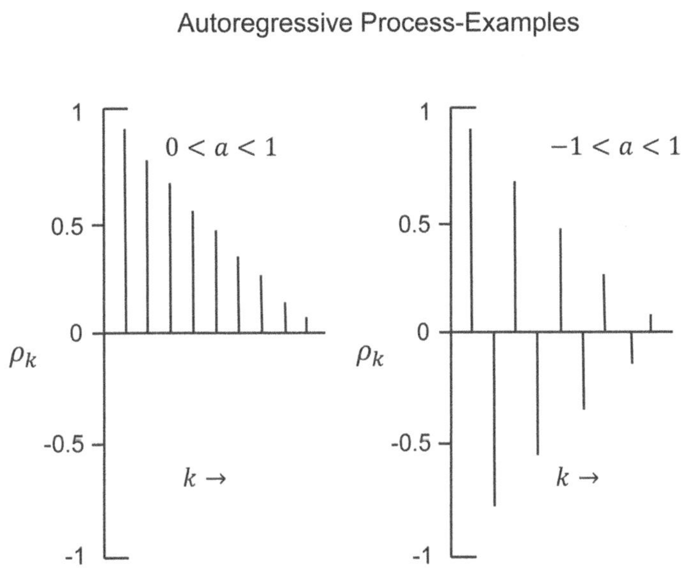

Figure A.3.1 Auto Correlation Function, Autoregressive Process-Examples

A special case where $a = 1$, is a realization of a process called the *random walk*. This process is given by:

$$y_t = y_{t-1} + \varepsilon_t$$

Each observation is given as follows:

$$y_t = y_{t-1} + \varepsilon_t$$
$$y_{t-1} = y_{t-2} + \varepsilon_{t-1}$$
$$\vdots$$
$$y_{t-k} = y_{t-k-1} + \varepsilon_{t-k}$$

By repeated substitutions, we obtain:

$$y_t = \sum_{i=1}^{k} \varepsilon_t$$

which has time dependent variance $\gamma_0 = t\sigma_\varepsilon^{\ 2}$, leading to the conclusion that the process is not stationary.

[Based on Mills, 1990; Box and Jenkins, 1970; Nelson, 1973; Nazem, 1988].

Second Order Autoregressive Process – AR(2)

This process is given by:

(29) $y_t = \alpha_1 y_{t-1} + \alpha_2 y_{t-2} + \varepsilon_t$, $t = 1, 2, \ldots T$, where ε_t is WN.

We can write this process as: $y_t = \dfrac{\varepsilon_t}{(1 - a_1 B - a_2 B^2)}$

Since we have a quadratic polynomial $(1 - a_1 B - a_2 B^2)$, we can rewrite it as:

$$1 - a_1 B - a_2 B^2 = (1 - \lambda_1 B)(1 - \lambda_2 B) = 1 - (\lambda_1 + \lambda_2)B + \lambda_1 \lambda_2 B^2$$

where we have $\lambda_1 + \lambda_2 = a_1$ and $-\lambda_1 \lambda_2 = a_2$. Provided that $|\lambda_1| < 1$ and $|\lambda_2| < 1$, we can write (29) as:

(30) $$y_t = \frac{\varepsilon_t}{(1 - \lambda_1 B)(1 - \lambda_2 B)} = \varepsilon_t \left[1 + (\lambda_1 B) + (\lambda_1 B)^2 + \ldots\right] \overbrace{\left[1 + (\lambda_2 B) + (\lambda_2 B)^2 + \ldots\right]} =$$

$$= M \sum_{j=0}^{\infty} \lambda_1^i \varepsilon_{t-i}$$

Therefore, from (30) we have $E(y_t) = 0$

Variance of the process is given by:

(31) $$\gamma_0 = E(y_t^2) = E\left[y_t(\alpha_1 y_{t-1} + \alpha_2 y_{t-2} + \varepsilon_t)\right] =$$

$$= \alpha_1 \overbrace{E(y_t y_{t-1})}^{\gamma_1} + \alpha_2 \overbrace{E(y_t y_{t-2})}^{\gamma_2} + E(y_t \varepsilon_t) =$$

$$= \alpha_1 \gamma_1 + \alpha_2 \gamma_2 + E\left[(\alpha_1 y_{t-1} + \alpha_2 y_{t-2} + \varepsilon_t)\varepsilon_t\right] =$$

$$= a_1 \gamma_1 + a_2 \gamma_2 + \alpha_1 \overbrace{E(y_{t-1}\varepsilon_t)}^{=0} + \alpha_2 \overbrace{E(y_{t-2}\varepsilon_t)}^{=0} + E(\varepsilon_t^{\ 2}) =$$

$$= a_1\gamma_1 + a_2\gamma_2 + \sigma_\varepsilon^{\ 2}$$

The ACV function is given by:

$$(32)\quad \gamma_1 = E(y_t y_{t-1}) = E\left[(\alpha_1 y_{t-1} + \alpha_2 y_{t-2} + \varepsilon_t) y_{t-1}\right] =$$

$$= \alpha_1 E(y_{t-1}^2) + \alpha_2 E(y_{t-1} y_{t-2}) + E(\varepsilon_t y_{t-1}) = \alpha_1\gamma_0 + \alpha_2\gamma_1$$

$$(33)\quad \gamma_2 = E(y_t y_{t-2}) = E\left[(\alpha_1 y_{t-1} + \alpha_2 y_{t-2} + \varepsilon_t) y_{t-2}\right] =$$

$$= \alpha_1 E(y_{t-1} y_{t-2}) + \alpha_2 E(y_{t-2}^2) + E(\varepsilon_t y_{t-2}) = \alpha_1\gamma_1 + \alpha_2\gamma_0$$

The ACR function is given by:

$$(34)\quad \rho_1 = \alpha_1 + \alpha_2\rho_1 \text{ or } \rho_1 = \frac{a_1}{1-a_2}$$

$$(35)\quad \rho_2 = \alpha_1\rho_1 + \alpha_2 \text{ or } \rho_2 = \frac{a_1^{\ 2}}{1-a_2} + a_2$$

[Based on Mills, 1990; Box and Jenkins, 1970; Nelson, 1973; Nazem, 1988].

Relationship between AR(2) and MA(q)

From (25) which is given by: $(1 - a_1 B - a_2 B^2)(1 - b_1 B - b_2 B^2 - ... - b_q B^q) = 1$

$$1 - a_1 B - a_2 B^2 - b_1 B + a_1 b_1 B^2 + a_2 b_1 B^3 - b_2 B^2 + a_1 b_2 B^3 + a_2 b_2 B^4 -$$
$$- b_3 B^3 + a_1 b_3 B^4 + a_2 b_3 B^5 - b_4 B^4 + a_1 b_4 B^5 + a_2 b_4 B^6 + ... = 1$$

After algebraic manipulations we obtain:

$$B(-b_1 - a_1) + B^2(-a_2 + a_1 b_1 - b_2) + B^3(a_2 b_1 + a_1 b_2 - b_3) + B^4(a_2 b_2 + a_1 b_3 - b_4) + ... = 0$$

The following solutions are given next:

$$\left.\begin{array}{l} -b_1 - a_1 = 0 \\ -a_2 + a_1 b_1 - b_2 = 0 \\ a_2 b_1 + a_1 b_2 - b_3 = 0 \\ a_2 b_2 + a_1 b_3 - b_4 = 0 \\ \vdots \end{array}\right\} \Rightarrow \left.\begin{array}{l} b_1 = -a_1 \\ b_2 = -a_2 + a_1 b_1 \\ b_3 = a_2 b_1 + a_1 b_2 \\ b_4 = a_2 b_2 + a_1 b_3 \\ \vdots \end{array}\right\} \Rightarrow b_j = a_1 b_{j-1} + a_2 b_{j-2} \text{ for } j \geq 2$$

[Based on Nazem, 1988].

Stationarity Conditions for AR(2)

For example, for AR(1) process, stationarity is realized if $|a| < 1$,or equivalently, the solution of $1 - aB = 0$, which is a^{-1}, has to be bigger than one in absolute value.

We know that AR(2) process can be written as:

$$a_p(B)y_t = \varepsilon_t \text{ where } a_p(B) = 1 - a_1 B - a_2 B^2$$

In this case, stationarity is assumed if the roots of $(1 - a_1 B - a_2 B^2) = 0$, are bigger than one in absolute value (lie outside the unit circle). Simply put, the AR(2), solutions have to be obtained from the solution of the auxiliary equation $m^2 - a_1 m - a_2 = 0$.[2] For stationarity, it is necessary that roots of the auxiliary equation are less then unity in modulus, that is, $|m_1| < 1$ and $|m_2| < 1$. As a result it generates the following set of restrictions on a_1 and a_2:

$$a_1 + a_2 < 1$$
$$a_2 - a_1 < 1$$
$$|a_2| < 1$$

Proof

The roots of the auxiliary equation are given by:

$$m_1, m_2 = \left| \frac{-a_1 \pm \sqrt{a_1^2 + 4a_2}}{2} \right| < 1$$

Case 1

$a_1^2 + 4a_2 > 0$, then we obtain: $-1 < 0.5a_1 \pm 0.5\sqrt{a_1^2 + 4a_2} < 1 \Rightarrow$

$$\Rightarrow \overbrace{-1 - 0.5a_1 < -0.5\sqrt{a_1^2 + 4a_2}}^{(a^*)} \overbrace{< 0.5\sqrt{a_1^2 + 4a_2} < 1 - 0.5a_1}^{(b^*)}$$

$$(a^*)\ 1 + 0.5a_1 > 0.5\sqrt{a_1^2 + 4a_2} \Rightarrow 1 + a_1 + 0.25a_1^2 > 0.25a_1^2 + a_2 \Rightarrow$$

$$\Rightarrow a_2 - a_1 < 1$$

2 AR(2): $y_1 = \alpha_1 y_{t-1} + \alpha_2 y_{t-2} + \varepsilon_t \Rightarrow y_t = m^t$ is the solution of HDE $(1 - a_1 B - a_2 B^2) y_t = 0$ $\Rightarrow m^t - a_1 m^{t-1} - a_2 m^{t-2} = 0 \Rightarrow m^{t+2} - a_1 m^{t+1} - a_2 m^t = 0 \Rightarrow m^t (m^2 - a_1 m - a_2) = 0$.

$$(b^*)\ \ 1-0.5a_1 > 0.5\sqrt{a_1^2+4a_2} \Rightarrow 1-a_1+0.25a_1^2 > 0.25a_1^2+a_2 \Rightarrow$$

$$\Rightarrow a_1+a_2<1$$

Case 2

$a_1^2+4a_2=0$, then we obtain: $-1<0.5a_1<1 \Rightarrow -2<a_1<2$.

Case 3

$a_1^2+4a_2<0$, then we obtain: $g, g^* = 0.5a_1 \pm i\sqrt{-(a_1^2+4a_2)} =$

$= |S|\left[\cos(\theta) \pm i\sin(\theta)\right] = |S|e^{\pm i\theta}$, where

$|S| = \sqrt{0.25a_1^2+0.25(-a_1^2-4a_2)} = \sqrt{-a_2}$.

Since we are looking for $|g|<1$ and $|g^*|<1$ and with the fact that $|S| = \left(g\cdot g^*\right)^{0.5}$ we require that $|S| = \sqrt{-a_2}<1$, which is satisfied if $-a_2<1$.

General Autoregressive Process – AR(p) and Yule-Walker Equations

An important fact about AR process is that it is possible to obtain a set of linear equations that express the parameters of the model in terms of variance and ACR of the data. These linear equations are called Yule-Walker equations.

Consider the general AR(p) process given by

(36) $y_t = a_1y_{t-1} + a_2y_{t-2} + ...a_py_{t-p} + \varepsilon_t$, where ε_t is WN.

We know that $E(y_{t-k}\varepsilon_t)=0$ for $k>0$. Then, the ACV function is given as follows:

(37) $\gamma_k = E(y_ty_{t-k})) = E(a_1y_{t-1}y_{t-k} + a_2y_{t-2}y_{t-k} + ...a_py_{t-p}y_{t-k} + \varepsilon_ty_{t-k})=$

$= a_1\gamma_{k-1} + a_2\gamma_{k-2} + ...a_p\gamma_{k-p}$ for $k>0$

Dividing (37) by its variance, we obtain the Yule-Walker equations:

(38) $\rho_k = a_1\rho_{k-1} + a_2\rho_{k-2} + ...a_p\rho_{k-p}$ for $k>0$

For $k=0$, by using (37) we obtain the following equation:

(39) $\sigma_y^2 = a_1\gamma_{-1} + a_2\gamma_{-2} + ...a_p\gamma_{-p} + E(\varepsilon_ty_t)$

Since for ACV we have, $\gamma_{-s} = \gamma_s$, hence we can drop the minus signs from (39). To compute $E(\varepsilon_t y_t)$ we use (36) as follows:

(40) $$E(\varepsilon_t y_t) = E(a_1 y_{t-1}\varepsilon_t + a_2 y_{t-2}\varepsilon_t + ...a_p y_{t-p}\varepsilon_t + \varepsilon_t^2) = E(\varepsilon_t^2) = \sigma_\varepsilon{}^2$$

Finally, for $k = 0$ we obtain:

(41) $$\gamma_0 = \sigma_y^2 = a_1\gamma_1 + a_2\gamma_2 + ...a_p\gamma_p + \sigma_\varepsilon^2$$

and

(42) $$1 = a_1\rho_1 + a_2\rho_2 + ...a_p\rho_p + \frac{\sigma_\varepsilon^2}{\sigma_y^2}$$

or

$$\sigma_\varepsilon{}^2 = \sigma_y{}^2\left[1 - a_1\rho_1 - a_2\rho_2 - ... - a_1\rho_p\right]$$

Any AR process, that can be represented in terms of past disturbances i.e., $y_t = b_q(B)\varepsilon_t$, requires us to fulfill the following conditions:

a) $\sum_{j=0}^{\infty}\left|a_j\right| < \infty$ i.e., convergence of the coefficients.

b) $a_p(B)b_q(B) = 1$.

c) $1 - a_1B - a_2B^2 - ... - a_pB^p = 0$, in order to insure the stationarity of the process. Equivalently, we require that the roots of the auxiliary equation $m^p - a_1m^{p-1} - ... - a_p = 0$, are $\left|m_j\right| < 1$ for $j = 1, 2, ...p$.

[Based on Mills, 1990; Box and Jenkins, 1970; Nelson, 1973; Nazem, 1988].

Partial Autocorrelation (PACR) Function

In general, in AR processes ACR functions damp out. However, it is sometimes difficult to distinguish between models of *different orders*. This is the main reason for our interest of PACR, that is, the *identification* of the nature of a time series process.

In general, the PACRs can be derived from Yule-Walker equations that can be written in matrix form:

$$\begin{bmatrix} 1 & \rho_1 & \rho_2 & \dots & \rho_{k-2} & \rho_{k-1} \\ \rho_1 & 1 & \rho_1 & \cdots & \rho_{k-3} & \rho_{k-2} \\ \vdots & \vdots & \vdots & \vdots & \vdots & \vdots \\ \rho_{k-1} & \rho_{k-2} & \rho_{k-3} & \cdots & \rho_1 & 1 \end{bmatrix} \begin{bmatrix} a_{k1} \\ a_{k2} \\ \vdots \\ a_{kk} \end{bmatrix} = \begin{bmatrix} \rho_1 \\ \rho_2 \\ \vdots \\ \rho_k \end{bmatrix}$$

Where ρ_j is the ACR of order j and a_{kj} is the j'th PACR of the AR(k) process.

Applying Cramer's rule, a_{kk}, can be written as:[3]

$$a_{kk} = \frac{P_k^*}{P_k} \text{ where } P_k = \begin{bmatrix} 1 & \rho_1 & \rho_2 & \dots & \rho_{k-2} & \rho_{k-1} \\ \rho_1 & 1 & \rho_1 & \cdots & \rho_{k-3} & \rho_{k-2} \\ \vdots & \vdots & \vdots & \vdots & \vdots & \vdots \\ \rho_{k-1} & \rho_{k-2} & \rho_{k-3} & \cdots & \rho_1 & 1 \end{bmatrix} \text{ and } P_k^* = \begin{bmatrix} 1 & \rho_1 & \rho_2 & \dots & \rho_{k-2} & \rho_1 \\ \rho_1 & 1 & \rho_1 & \cdots & \rho_{k-3} & \rho_2 \\ \vdots & \vdots & \vdots & \vdots & \vdots & \vdots \\ \rho_{k-1} & \rho_{k-2} & \rho_{k-3} & \cdots & \rho_1 & \rho_k \end{bmatrix}$$

Note that P_k^* is the same as P_k, except that the last column is replaced by a column vector composed of all ACR coefficients.

For example a_{11}, a_{22} and a_{33} can be expressed as follows:[4]

$$a_{11} = \frac{[\rho_1]}{[1]} = \rho_1, \quad a_{22} = \frac{\begin{bmatrix} 1 & \rho_1 \\ \rho_1 & \rho_2 \end{bmatrix}}{\begin{bmatrix} 1 & \rho_1 \\ \rho_1 & 1 \end{bmatrix}} = \frac{\rho_2 - \rho_1^2}{1 - \rho_1^2}, \quad a_{33} = \frac{\begin{bmatrix} 1 & \rho_1 & \rho_1 \\ \rho_1 & 1 & \rho_2 \\ \rho_2 & \rho_1 & \rho_3 \end{bmatrix}}{\begin{bmatrix} 1 & \rho_1 & \rho_2 \\ \rho_1 & 1 & \rho_1 \\ \rho_2 & \rho_1 & 1 \end{bmatrix}} = \frac{\rho_3 - 2\rho_1\rho_2 - \rho_1^2\rho_3 + \rho_1\rho_2^2 + \rho_1^3}{1 - 2\rho_1^2 + 2\rho_1^2\rho_2 - \rho_2^2}$$

We have shown the technique for computing the partial autocorrelations for lower orders. However, it is unlikely that anyone would even attempt to estimate higher order partial autocorrelations without a computer.

In general, MA and AR processes are considered *dual* processes. Just as ACR function damps out for a finite order AR process and cuts off for a finite order MA process, the reverse is true for the PACR function. This can be summarized in the following table:

---

3 See Lipschutz, S., *Theory and Problems of Beginning Linear Algebra, 1997.*

4 The determinant of the 3x3 matrix can be rewritten as follows:

$$A = \begin{bmatrix} a_{11} & a_{12} & a_{13} \\ a_{21} & a_{22} & a_{23} \\ a_{31} & a_{32} & a_{33} \end{bmatrix} \Rightarrow \det(A) = a_{11}(a_{22}a_{33} - a_{23}a_{32}) - a_{12}(a_{21}a_{33} - a_{23}a_{31}) + a_{11}(a_{21}a_{32} - a_{22}a_{31})$$

Functions		
Process	ACR	PACR
AR	Damps Out	Cuts Off
MA	Cuts Off	Damps Out

In practice, PACRs are always subject to sampling errors. Quenouille (1949) proved that PACRs are approximately *normally distributed*, with a *mean zero* and *variance equal to the inverse of the size of the sample.*

[Based on Nazem, 1988].

Autoregressive Moving Average (ARMA) Process

Many time series can be realized by more complex structural relationships. Typically, such models include both AR and MA components.

ARMA(1,1) Process

This process is given by:

(43) $y_t = \alpha y_{t-1} + \varepsilon_t - b\varepsilon_{t-1}$, where ε_t is WN.

This model can be rewritten as:

$$y_t = \frac{1-bB}{1-aB}\varepsilon_t$$

where $(1-aB)(1+u_1B+u_2B^2+...)=1-bB$, which leads to a MA($\infty$) representation:

$$y_t = \sum_{j=0}^{\infty} u_j \varepsilon_{t-j}$$

Alternatively we can rewrite the model as follows:

$$\varepsilon_t = \frac{1-aB}{1-bB} y_t$$

where $(1-bB)(1+w_1B+w_2B^2+...)=1-aB$, which leads to an AR($\infty$) representation as follows:

$$\varepsilon_t = \sum_{j=0}^{\infty} w_j y_{t-j}$$

The "u"-weights in the MA(∞) representation, after algebraic manipulations are given as follows:

$$\left.\begin{aligned} u_1 - a &= -b \\ u_2 - au_1 &= 0 \\ &\vdots \\ u_j - au_{j-1} &= 0 \end{aligned}\right\} \Rightarrow \left.\begin{aligned} u_1 &= a - b \\ u_2 &= au_1 = a(a-b) \\ &\vdots \\ u_j &= au_{j-1} = a^{j-1}(a-b) \end{aligned}\right\}$$

Similarly with respect to the "w"-weights in AR(∞) representation; the following is obtained:

$$\left.\begin{aligned} -w_1 - b &= -a \\ -w_2 + bw_1 &= 0 \\ &\vdots \\ -w_j + bu_{j-1} &= 0 \end{aligned}\right\} \Rightarrow \left.\begin{aligned} w_1 &= a - b \\ w_2 &= bw_1 = b(a-b) \\ &\vdots \\ w_j &= bw_{j-1} = b^{j-1}(a-b) \end{aligned}\right\}$$

We can see that the "u"-weights in the MA(∞) representation *converge* for $|a| < 1$, satisfying the *stationarity* condition. Likewise, the "w"-weights converge for $|b| < 1$, satisfying the *invertibility* condition.

The model given by (43) can be written as $y_t - \alpha y_{t-1} = \varepsilon_t - b\varepsilon_{t-1}$. Multiplying both sides by y_{t-k} and taking expectations gives us:

(44) $\gamma_k - \alpha\gamma_{k-1} = E(\varepsilon_t y_{t-k}) - bE(\varepsilon_{t-1} y_{t-k})$

For $k > 1$ $E(\varepsilon_t y_{t-k}) = E(\varepsilon_{t-1} y_{t-k}) = 0$ since ε_t and ε_{t-1} are uncorrelated with. Therefore, we obtain $\gamma_k - \alpha\gamma_{k-1} = 0$, for $k > 1$.

Since $y_t = \sum_{j=0}^{\infty} u\varepsilon_{t-j}$ it is easy to find that:

$E(\varepsilon_t y_t) = E(\varepsilon_{t-1} y_{t-1}) = \sigma^2$ and $E(\varepsilon_{t-1} y_t) = u_1\sigma^2 = (a-b)\sigma^2$.[5]

Given (44), for $k = 0$ and $k = 1$, we obtain the next system of equations:

---

5 For example: $E(\varepsilon_t y_t) = E[\varepsilon_t u(B)\varepsilon_t] = E[\varepsilon_t(\varepsilon_t + u_1\varepsilon_{t-1} + u_2\varepsilon_{t-2} + \ldots)] = E(\varepsilon_t^2) + E(CPT) = \sigma^2$.

$$\begin{cases} \gamma_0 - \alpha\gamma_1 = \sigma^2 - b(a-b)\sigma^2 \\ \gamma_1 - \alpha\gamma_0 = -b\sigma^2 \end{cases} \Rightarrow \begin{cases} \gamma_0 = \dfrac{(1+b^2-2ab)\sigma^2}{1-a^2} \\ \gamma_1 = \dfrac{(1-ab)(a-b)\sigma^2}{1-a^2} \end{cases}$$

The ACR function is given by:

$$\rho_1 = \frac{(1-ab)(a-b)}{1+b^2-2ab} \text{ and } \rho_k = \alpha\rho_{k-1}, \text{ for } k > 1.$$

The PACR is computed by the method we have shown before, that is:

$$a_{kk} = \frac{P_k^*}{P_k} \text{ which yields for example } a_{11} = \frac{[\rho_1]}{[1]} = \rho_1 \text{ and } a_{22} = \frac{\begin{bmatrix} 1 & \rho_1 \\ \rho_1 & \rho_2 \end{bmatrix}}{\begin{bmatrix} 1 & \rho_1 \\ \rho_1 & 1 \end{bmatrix}} = \frac{\rho_2 - \rho_1^2}{1-\rho_1^2}$$

where ρ_1 and ρ_2 are represented in terms of model parameters.

[Based on Mills, 1990; Box and Jenkins, 1970; Nelson, 1973; Nazem, 1988].

General ARMA(p,q) Process

This process is given by:

(45) $y_t = \alpha_1 y_{t-1} + \alpha_2 y_{t-2} + \ldots + a_p y_{t-p} \ldots + \varepsilon_t - b_1\varepsilon_{t-1} - b_2\varepsilon_{t-2} - \ldots b_q\varepsilon_{t-q}$.

The pure MA(∞) representation is given by $y_t = u_q(B)\varepsilon_t$, where $u_q(B) = \dfrac{b(B)}{a(B)}$.

The pure AR(∞) representation is given by $\varepsilon_t = w_p(B)y_t$ where $w_p(B) = \dfrac{a(B)}{b(B)}$.

The "u" and "w" weights can be derived from the following relationship $w_p(B) = u_q^{-1}(B)$. For stationarity, the roots of $a_p(B) = 0$ must lie outside the unit circle, and for invertibility the roots of $b_q(B) = 0$ must also lie outside the unit circle.

The ACV function is given by:

$$\gamma_k = E(y_t y_{t-k}) = E(a_1 y_{t-1} y_{t-k} + \ldots + a_p y_{t-p} y_{t-k} + b_1 \varepsilon_t y_{t-k} + \ldots + b_q \varepsilon_{t-q} y_{t-k}).$$

We must note that there are *two cases* which have to be checked (Nelson, 1973).

Case 1

If $k < q$, then the terms involving y_{t-k} and past disturbances will be nonzero, since y_{t-k} is correlated with all disturbances occurring through period $t-k$. Therefore, the ACV equations will include MA parameters i.e., $b_1, b_2, \ldots b_q$.

Case 2

If $k > q$, then we simply have $\gamma_k = a_1\gamma_{k-1} + a_2\gamma_{k-2} + \ldots a_p\gamma_{k-p}$ and consequently the ACR is $\rho_k = a_1\rho_{k-1} + a_2\rho_{k-2} + \ldots a_p\rho_{k-p}$.

[Based on Mills, 1990; Box and Jenkins, 1970; Nelson, 1973; Nazem, 1988].

Non-Stationary Time Series

The class of ARMA models relies on the assumption that the underlying process is stationary. However, in practice most time series are non-stationary, in particular, they behave *as if* there is no fixed mean and variance. In order to fit a stationary model, it is necessary to remove the non-stationary sources of variation. Thus, it may be the case that differencing the time series is necessary, and therefore, the model can be represented by ARMA(p,q).

The Degree of Differencing

Generally, when we deal with observed time series y_t from a non-stationary process we should follow a number of steps:

a) Create a *first difference series*, which is defined as follows:

$$w_1 = y_2 - y_1$$
$$w_2 = y_3 - y_2$$
$$\vdots$$
$$w_{t-1} = y_t - y_{t-1}$$

b) If the first difference series is still non-stationary, then another differencing is necessary:

$$z_1 = w_2 - w_1 = y_3 - 2y_2 + y_1$$
$$z_2 = w_3 - w_2 = y_4 - 2y_3 + y_2$$
$$\vdots$$
$$z_{t-2} = w_t - w_{t-1} = y_t - 2y_{t-1} + y_{t-2}$$

Generally, differencing more than twice is rare in time series related to economic and business data.

The classes of time series models, which are based on differencing procedures, are called *integrated time series models*.[6] If such a model includes *only* MA or *only* AR components, then it will be called an *integrated moving average* (IMA) or an *integrated autoregressive* (ARI) *model*, respectively. The class of mixed models which include *both* MA and AR components are called *autoregressive integrated moving average* (ARIMA) models, or more precisely ARIMA(p,d,q), where *p, d* and *q* are orders of AR process, degree of differencing and MA process, respectively.

General ARIMA(p,d,q) Process

Consider the process which is given by:

(46) $c(B)y_t = b(B)\varepsilon_t$, where ε_t is WN.

a) $c_p(B)$ is an AR operator. It is assumed to be *non-stationary* such that d of the roots of $c_q(B) = 0$ are unity.

b) $b_q(B)$ is a MA operator. It is assumed to be invertible such that the roots of $b_q(B) = 0$ lie outside the unit circle.

Then by differencing we can transform (46) into:

(48) $(1 - a_1 B - \ldots - a_p B^p)(1-B)^d y_t = (1 - b_1 B - \ldots - b_q B^q)\varepsilon_t$

which can be shortly written in short as $a_p(B)\nabla^d y_t = b_q(B)\varepsilon_t$, where:

c) $a_p(B)$ is an AR operator. It is assumed to be stationary such that the roots of $a_p(B) = 0$ lie outside the unit circle.

---

6 The title "integrated time series models" suggests that these models are described by a process of integration of differenced series.

If we define $w_t = \nabla^d y_t$, then (48) can be given as $a(B)w_t = b_q(B)\varepsilon_t$. Therefore, for $d \geq 1$ the latter representation is simply an invertible and stationary ARMA(p,q) process.

[Based on Mills, 1990; Box and Jenkins, 1970; Nelson, 1973; Nazem, 1988].

INDEX